pathfinder guide

Heart of England

WALKS

Compiled by
Brian Conduit

Acknowledgements
I am grateful to the following for their advice and assistance:
Mr C. Robinson (Forestry Commission), Mr J. Shryane
(Staffordshire County Council), Mr T. Hughes (Shropshire
County Council), Mr V.E. Jones (Hereford and Worcester
County Council), Mr S. Ikeringill (Warwickshire County
Council), Mr D.L. Judge (Malvern Hills Conservators) and
Mr C.W. Rolfe (National Trust, Mercia Regional Office).

Text:	Brian Conduit
Photography:	Brian Conduit and
	Jarrold Publishing
Editors:	Donald Greig, Chris Goddard
Designers:	Brian Skinner, Doug Whitworth
Mapping:	Heather Pearson, Sandy Sims

Series Consultant: Brian Conduit

© Jarrold Publishing and Ordnance Survey 1993, 1996
Maps © Crown copyright 1996. The mapping in this guide is
based upon Ordnance Survey ® Pathfinder ®, Outdoor Leisure
™, Explorer ™ and Travelmaster ® mapping. Ordnance Survey,
Pathfinder and Travelmaster are registered trade marks and
Outdoor Leisure and Explorer are trade marks of Ordnance
Survey, the National Mapping Agency of Great Britain.

Jarrold Publishing   ISBN 0-7117-0570-4

First published 1992
by Jarrold Publishing and Ordnance Survey

Printed in Great Britain
by Jarrold Book Printing, Thetford. 2/97

Jarrold Publishing,
Whitefriars, Norwich NR3 1TR
Ordnance Survey,
Romsey Road, Southampton SO16 4GU

Front cover:	View from the Clent Hills
Previous page:	Old houses in Alcester

Contents

Contents

Short, easy walks

Walks of modest length, likely to involve some modest uphill walking

More challenging walks which may be longer and/or over more rugged terrain, often with some stiff climbs

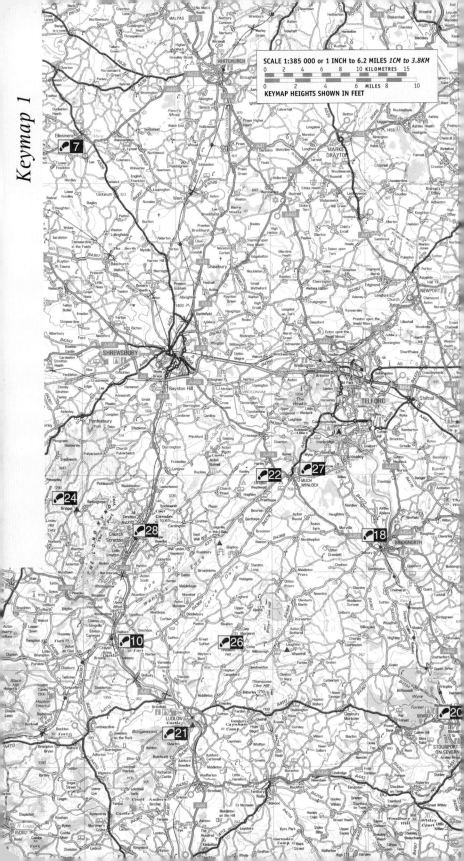

Keymap 1

SCALE 1:385 000 or 1 INCH to 6.2 MILES *1CM to 3.8KM*

KEYMAP HEIGHTS SHOWN IN FEET

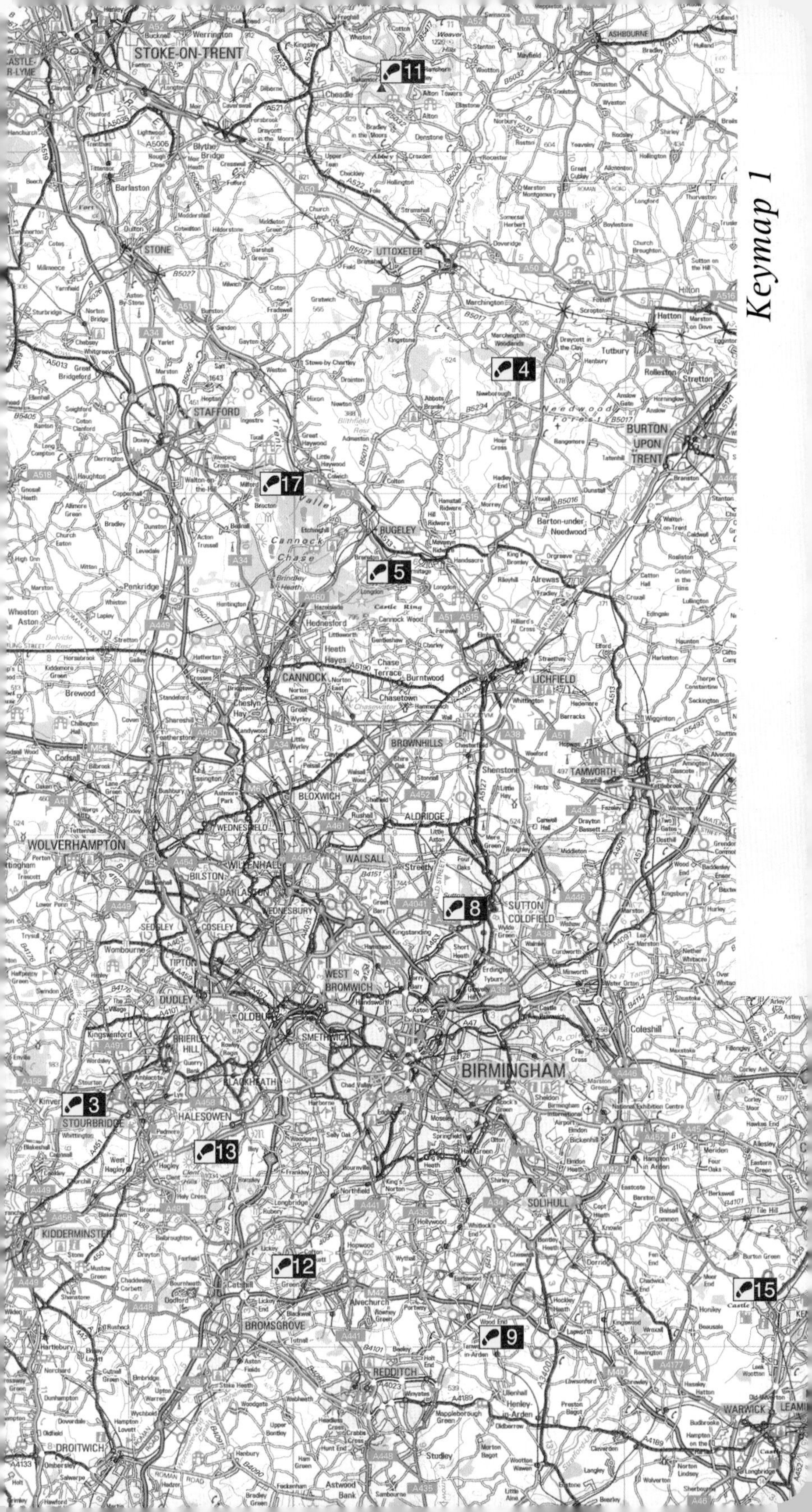

STOKE-ON-TRENT

11

STAFFORD

4

17

RUGELEY

5

CANNOCK

UTTOXETER

BURTON UPON TRENT

LICHFIELD

BROWNHILLS

TAMWORTH

ALDRIDGE

WALSALL

WOLVERHAMPTON

8

SUTTON COLDFIELD

DUDLEY

OLDBURY

WEST BROMWICH

SMETHWICK

BIRMINGHAM

3

STOURBRIDGE

HALESOWEN

13

KIDDERMINSTER

SOLIHULL

12

15

BROMSGROVE

9

DROITWICH

REDDITCH

WARWICK

LEAM

Keymap 2

Keymap 2

Walk	Page	Start	Distance	Time
Alcester and Wixford	16	Alcester	5 miles (8km)	2½ hrs
Bewdley and Wyre Forest	61	Bewdley	8 miles (12.9km)	4 hrs
Bidford-on-Avon, Cleeve Prior and Middle Littleton	58	Bidford-on-Avon	8 miles (12.9km)	4 hrs
Bridgnorth and the River Severn	55	Bridgnorth	8½ miles (13.7km)	4½ hrs
Brown Clee Hill	80	North of Stoke St Milborough	7½ miles (12.1km)	3½ hrs
Castlemorton Common and the British Camp	70	On A449 south of Great Malvern	7 miles (11.3km)	3½ hrs
Churnet Valley and Alton	36	Oakamoor	6 miles (9.7km)	3 hrs
Clent Hills	42	Clent Hills – Nimmings Lane Visitor Centre	5½ miles (8.9km)	3 hrs
Ellesmere Lakes	26	Ellesmere	6½ miles (10.5km)	3½ hrs
Great Malvern and the Worcestershire Beacon	50	Great Malvern	5½ miles (8.9km)	3 hrs
Henley-in-Arden and Preston Bagot	24	Henley-in-Arden	5 miles (8 km)	2½ hrs
Kenilworth and Honiley	47	Kenilworth	6½ miles (10.5km)	3½ hrs
Kinver Edge	18	Kinver	4½ miles (7.2km)	2½ hrs
Lickey Hills	39	Lickey Hills Visitor Centre	5½ miles (8.9km)	3 hrs
The Long Mynd	87	Church Stretton	8 miles (12.9km)	4 hrs
Ludlow, Bromfield and Bringewood Chase	64	Ludlow	9 miles (14.5km)	4½ hrs
Marquis Drive and Castle Ring	22	Brereton Spurs picnic area	5 miles (8km)	2½ hrs
Much Wenlock, Ironbridge Gorge and Buildwas Park	83	Much Wenlock	11½ miles (18.5km)	6 hrs
Needwood Forest	20	South-west of Draycott in the Clay	5 miles (8km)	2½ hrs
Shakespeare Country	76	Stratford-upon-Avon	10 miles (16km)	5 hrs
Shugborough Park, Sherbrook Valley and Brocton Coppice	52	Milford Common	7 miles (11.3km)	3½ hrs
Stiperstones	73	Bridges	7 miles (11.3km)	3½ hrs
Stokesay Castle and View Wood	34	Stokesay Castle	5½ miles (8.9km)	3 hrs
Sutton Park	28	Sutton Park Visitor Centre	6½ miles (10.5km)	3½ hrs
Tanworth-in-Arden	31	Tanworth-in-Arden	6½ miles (10.5km)	3½ hrs
Tyddesley Wood and the River Avon	14	Pershore	5 miles (8km)	2½ hrs
Wenlock Edge	67	Wenlock Edge	8 miles (12.9km)	4 hrs
Witley Court and Abberley Hill	44	Great Witley	6½ miles (10.5km)	3½ hrs

The line of the old Roman road of Ryknild Street is followed on the return stretch of this easy walk in the countryside of Arden.

This walk takes you along paths and tracks through the woodlands of Wyre Forest, and there are several fine views over the Severn valley. Expect some muddy stretches in places.

For almost 3 miles (4.8km) you follow a low ridge above the River Avon from which there are fine views across the Vale of Evesham to the Cotswolds and Malverns.

The latter part of the walk follows a most attractive path beside the River Severn to return to Bridgnorth.

The highest point both in Shropshire and the 'Heart of England' as a whole inevitably provides extensive views. There is some rough and boggy terrain near the summit.

A walk across Castlemorton Common below the Malverns is followed by a steady climb to the Herefordshire Beacon, which is both a superb viewpoint and the site of an Iron Age fort.

The landscape of the wooded, steep-sided Churnet valley has been compared with that of Switzerland. A disused railway track is followed on the second half of the walk.

The ridge walks and modest gradients of the Clent Hills on the edge of the Black Country give splendid views over Worcestershire and Shropshire.

A highly distinctive and almost entirely flat walk in the 'mere country' around Ellesmere in north Shropshire.

The route contours around the slopes of the Malverns to reach the Worcestershire Beacon, the highest point on those hills, giving a succession of magnificent views.

The hilly sections of the walk are near the start; after that come relaxing strolls first by the Stratford-upon-Avon Canal and later by the River Alne.

Most of this walk is along clear and well-waymarked field paths with the majestic ruins of Kenilworth Castle in sight for much of the way.

There are grand views and pleasant woodland walking to be enjoyed from the wooded escarpment of Kinver Edge, a popular beauty spot.

Rising to just under 1000ft, the well-wooded Lickey Hills on the south-western fringes of Birmingham have long been a favourite weekend venue.

The initial climb up the narrow Carding Mill Valley provides a fine introduction to the magnificent ridge walk along the top of the Long Mynd.

The walk is mostly through parkland and woodland with fine views of the River Teme. Near the end comes a spectacular view over Ludlow and the Clee Hills.

Clear tracks through woodland and across heath lead to Castle Ring, the highest point in Cannock Chase, with fine views over the Trent valley.

A fascinating walk that combines two medieval monastic ruins with the world-famous industrial monuments of the Ironbridge Gorge.

This walk explores some of the few surviving woodlands of the once extensive royal forest of Needwood.

Villages of half-timbered and thatched cottages, medieval churches and a lovely finale beside the River Avon add up to a memorable walk in the heart of Shakespeare Country.

Plenty of both scenic and historic variety can be enjoyed on this walk that takes you through the finest surviving portions of Cannock Chase.

You could almost imagine that you were in parts of the Pennines rather than the Welsh border country as you walk past the jagged pinnacles and shattered rocks of the Stiperstones.

There are some fine, wooded stretches and extensive views over the lovely Welsh border country.

Thick woodland, open heathland and a series of pools provide real country walking within the boundaries of Britain's second city.

An attractive village is the starting point for this walk in the still well-wooded countryside of the Forest of Arden. Parts could be muddy after rain.

Woodland, views of Bredon Hill and an attractive stroll by the River Avon are the chief delights of this short walk.

Enjoy the grand views across to the Long Mynd and the Wrekin from the thickly wooded ridge of Wenlock Edge.

A short but fairly steep climb up the wooded slopes of Abberley Hill is followed by a superb ridge-top walk.

At-a-glance...

Introduction to
the Heart of England

'Heart of England' is as much an emotional as a geographical term. The image that it conjures up is of a largely unchanged, unspoilt, rural landscape of farmland and woodland, through which flow slowly meandering rivers, and which is dotted with small market towns and sleepy villages of thatched and half-timbered cottages, welcoming inns and old churches; the landscape that inspired, among others, William Shakespeare and Edward Elgar; a landscape in which beats the true 'heart' of England. Despite the industrialisation and urban expansion of the last 200 years and the recent creation of a busy motorway network, this image still manages to hold true in many parts of the region.

Geographically, 'Heart of England' is an imprecise term referring to Middle England, necessarily vague because Middle England has no clearly defined limits. The Anglo-Saxon kingdom of Mercia never had precise boundaries but sprawled over Middle England, at times embracing East Anglia and reaching as far as the Thames in the south and Ribble in the north. Only in the west did Mercia have a definite and unmistakable frontier, the 80-mile (130km) dyke built by Offa the Great to mark the border between his kingdom and the territories of the Welsh princes. Walking guides, however, require some geographical limits and here it is defined as the counties of Shropshire, Staffordshire, Warwickshire, West Midlands and the Worcestershire half of Hereford and Worcester.

Scenic and Historic Contrasts

If you stand on one of the prominent all-round viewpoints in the centre of the Heart of England, such as the Four Stones on the Clent Hills or the summit of Beacon Hill, you get some idea of the tremendous scenic and historic contrasts of the area. Spread out before you is a gently rolling patchwork of fields, hedgerows and woodland stretching away to the distant outlines of the Shropshire, Cotswold and Malvern Hills. But in addition the extensive views encompass part of the densely populated and highly industrialised Black Country and look across the tower blocks of Birmingham, not only revealing the close juxtaposition of industrial and rural landscapes in this region, but also clearly indicating that this is the heart of industrial England. As a consequence both of this and of its central location, the area also became the heart of the country's transport system – first of canals, then railways and more recently motorways.

Indeed, the Ironbridge Gorge in Shropshire proudly claims to be the 'birthplace of the Industrial Revolution' and, in recognition of its unique significance and early industrial monuments, it has been designated a

World Heritage Site. It was here at his Coalbrookdale works that Abraham Darby revolutionised the iron industry, and thereby industry as a whole, by his success in smelting iron ore with coke instead of charcoal, thus freeing the industry from its dependence upon the nation's rapidly dwindling timber resources and enabling it to expand. The world's first iron bridge, probably Britain's finest and best-known industrial monument, was also built here, across the River Severn. The Ironbridge Gorge had a relatively short history as a major industrial area; industry later moved closer to the abundant coal supplies of south Staffordshire. During the 19th century, the vast amount of smoke that poured into the atmosphere from the numerous furnaces and forges of that area earned for it the nickname 'Black Country' – undeniably deserved as late as the 1950s but, as a result of clean air legislation and the decline of traditional industry, no longer true today.

Abraham Darby's invention had an important, if no doubt unintentional, side-effect. As timber was no longer needed by the Midland ironmasters, it helped to preserve some of the woodlands and forests, remnants of an older landscape of forest and heath that once covered much of the Heart of England. Over the centuries these forests gradually diminished and in some cases almost vanished, initially to make way for the steady but unrelenting encroachment of agriculture, later to serve the needs of the navy as well as the local iron industries, and ultimately to clear the way for urban and industrial growth. Nevertheless, splendid and extensive areas survive in Cannock Chase, Wyre Forest and Sutton Park and, together with smaller and separate remnants of the forests of Needwood and Shakespeare's Arden, they enable us to appreciate how large parts of the Midlands, and indeed lowland England in general, would have looked in the Middle Ages.

The woodland areas also provide superb walking country, part of the wide variety of terrain to be found in the Heart of England. Within the county of Shropshire alone there is an infinite choice. Ramblers head mainly for the hills of south Shropshire, to enjoy the magnificent views from the four great ridges of Wenlock Edge, Long Mynd, Stiperstones and the Clee Hills, views that extend eastwards over the Midland plain and westwards across to Wales. These ridges provide not only the roughest and wildest country to be encountered by the walker in the Heart of England but also the loftiest; at 1771ft (540m), Brown Clee Hill is the highest point in the region covered by this walking guide.

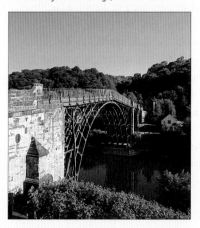

The world's first iron bridge, built in 1779

This area of Shropshire was part of the Welsh Marches and still has the feel of border country, especially around the former walled towns and ruined medieval fortresses of Ludlow and Bridgnorth, and the highly photogenic fortified manor house of Stokesay Castle, just outside Craven Arms. But there is a more peaceful and gentle side to Shropshire as well: the mellowed monastic remains at Much Wenlock and Buildwas, quiet riverside walking by the Severn and, in the flatter northern half of the county, the collection of tree-fringed lakes around Ellesmere. To complete the county's varied attractions, there is the different scenic and historic environment of the Ironbridge Gorge, where a fascinating series of monuments of the Industrial Revolution are presided over by the distinctive, conical-shaped bulk of the Wrekin.

For those who think of Staffordshire mainly in terms of the Potteries and Black Country, some pleasant surprises await. In the south-west of the county the densely wooded slopes of Kinver Edge give grand views over the surrounding countryside to the hills of Worcestershire and Shropshire. Sandwiched between the Black Country, M6, Stafford and the Trent valley lies Cannock Chase, which in Saxon times was a royal forest and later the private hunting-ground of the medieval bishops of Lichfield. Although much of it now consists of conifer plantations, it is excellent walking country, containing the largest area of open heathland left in the Heart of England and still retaining some ancient oak woodlands near Brocton and Milford. Further north, between the Trent and Dove and set amidst quiet farming country, are the detached woodlands of the former royal forest of Needwood and, still further north, the steep and thickly wooded slopes of the Churnet valley look northwards to the moorlands on the fringes of the Peak District, frontier country between the Heart of England and the north.

Worcestershire is as varied as Shropshire and, although its hills may be lower and less wild, the Worcestershire Beacon in the Malverns, the highest point in the county, does rise to 1395ft (425m). The Malvern Hills stand out so boldly above the surrounding landscape that they have the appearance of a mountain range, and the views from the lengthy switchback ridge – westwards across the undulating country of Herefordshire to the Welsh hills, southwards towards the Forest of Dean and eastwards over the Vale of Severn to the Cotswold escarpment – are among the most spectacular, extensive and rewarding in the country. This is 'Elgar country': the great composer was born nearby, spent most of his life in the shadow of the Malverns, loved to walk on the hills and is buried just below them.

To the north and north-east of the Malverns are other – smaller and lower – ranges of hills that provide more fine walking and dramatic ridgetop views. The well-wooded Abberley Hills lie between the Severn and Teme valleys and look northwards towards Wyre Forest; to the east of the River Severn the more bare and open slopes of the Clent Hills just attain the 1000ft (305m) mark, while the nearby Lickey Hills, traditional weekend playground for the people of Birmingham, almost reach the same heights.

In south Worcestershire the River Avon winds gently through the flat orchard and market-gardening country of the Vale of Evesham. This is a countryside of wide horizons and attractive thatched stone and half-timbered cottages, overlooked by Bredon Hill and the western edge of the Cotswolds: another kind of frontier zone, this time between the Heart of England and the south.

From the Vale of Evesham, the Avon continues northwards and eastwards into Warwickshire, through an area known the world over by the name of England's greatest dramatist and Warwickshire's most famous son. Shakespeare Country stretches northwards from the Avon valley

Stokesay Castle - fortified manor house near the Welsh border

through the still well-wooded land of Arden; a gently rolling countryside – interspersed with old market towns, 'chocolate-box' villages and picturesque black-and-white farmhouses and cottages – that hardly seems to have changed since Tudor times. To many visitors this may well be the landscape that comes closest to their expectations of the Heart of England.

Heart of the Path Network

Walking in the region is generally trouble-free, with mostly clear paths, good waymarking and a number of long-distance footpaths. Kinver Edge is the meeting-point for three of the latter: the Staffordshire Way, which runs northwards to Cannock Chase and on through the Trent, Dove and Churnet valleys to the Cheshire border; the North Worcestershire Path, which heads eastwards to link together the Kingsford, Clent Hills, Waseley Hills and Lickey Hills country parks; and the Worcestershire Way, which leads southwards to the Severn valley, then over the Abberley Hills and on to the Malverns. In addition there are: the Shropshire Way, which snakes across the county linking all the main walking areas; the Wychavon Way, which runs across Worcestershire from the River Severn to the Cotswolds; and finally the Heart of England Way itself, which connects Cannock Chase with the Cotswolds. All these paths link with each other and with other long-distance routes (Offa's Dyke Path, Cotswold Way) to bestow on the Heart of England a new role, as the hub or 'heart' of the country's extensive and ever-growing network of long-distance paths.

Tyddesley Wood and the River Avon

Start	Pershore
Distance	5 miles (8km)
Approximate time	2½ hours
Parking	Pershore
Refreshments	Pubs and cafés at Pershore
Ordnance Survey maps	Landranger 150 (Worcester & The Malverns) and Explorer 14 (Malvern Hills)

This gentle stroll in the fruit-growing and market-gardening country of the Vale of Evesham includes fine woodland and views of the distinctive bulk of Bredon Hill, finishing with a most attractive walk across flat meadowland by the River Avon. For much of the way the tower of Pershore Abbey is in sight.

Situated amidst orchards and water-meadows bordering the River Avon, Pershore is a pleasant town of dignified Georgian buildings dominated by the tower of its abbey church. The 14th-century tower, together with the 13th-century east end and transepts, are the only parts of the Benedictine monastery that survived Henry VIII's destruction in the 1530s, but they are nonetheless a most impressive remnant.

Start in the town centre, at the junction of Broad Street and Bridge Street, by walking along Broad Street. At the end, cross the road and take the tarmac path ahead across Abbey Park, bearing right to pass in front of the abbey along the right-hand side of a hedge bordering a bowling green, then bearing left along a paved path. Cross a road, continue along the tarmac path opposite (to the right of a school entrance), bending right and left to a road. Keep ahead along New Road, cross the main road **Ⓐ** and continue along Holloway, heading gently uphill.

After nearly ½ mile (800m) turn left, at a public footpath sign **Ⓑ**, along a straight track between fields, from which there are fine open views: the Malverns to the right, Bredon Hill and Pershore to the left and

Springtime in Tyddesley Wood, near Pershore

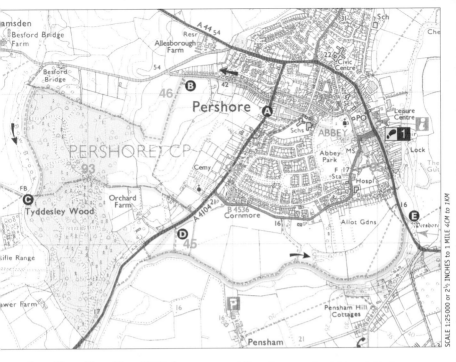

| 0 | 200 | 400 | 600 | 800 METRES | 1 | |
| 0 | 200 | 400 | 600 YARDS | ½ | | |

KILOMETRES
MILES

Tyddesley Wood ahead. Just in front of a small clump of trees, turn right on to a clear path which heads towards Tyddesley Wood, turning right and shortly left to head downhill along the right-hand edge of the wood. Climb a stile, keep along the edge of the wood and climb two more stiles; after the second, crossing a track and continuing along a delightful tree-lined path which is just inside the edge of the wood.

At the corner of the wood do not climb the stile in front, but turn left over another stile to continue along the bottom edge of the wood, by young orchards on the right. Where the edge of the wood bends to the right, turn left over a stile **C**, keep ahead a few yards and then bear left to follow a broad green track through Tyddesley Wood, a most attractive area of mixed woodland. Cross a stony track, keep ahead and climb a stile to emerge from the wood. Now continue along the right-hand edge of a field, by a wire fence

and line of trees on the right, and climb two stiles in quick succession, then keep along the left-hand edge of a field, by a hedge on the left. Just before reaching a stile at the end of the field, bear right and head down towards a thatched black-and-white cottage, climbing a stile and continuing along the tarmac drive ahead to a road.

Turn right and, at a public footpath sign, turn left over a stile **D** to follow the left-hand edge of a field, by a wire fence and trees on the left, down to the river. Turn left to cross a footbridge over a ditch, and now comes a particularly pleasant part of the walk across riverside meadows by the placid waters of the Avon, crossing over several stiles and footbridges, with attractive views of Bredon Hill to the right and the tower of Pershore Abbey to the left. Follow the river around a left curve to a bridge and then go up steps on to the road **E**. Ahead is the picturesque bridge built during the 14th-century by the monks of Pershore Abbey. Turn left in order to return to the town centre.

Alcester and Wixford

Start	Alcester
Distance	5 miles (8km). Shorter version 4 miles (6.4km)
Approximate time	2½ hours (2 hours for shorter version)
Parking	Alcester
Refreshments	Pubs and cafés at Alcester, pub at Wixford
Ordnance Survey maps	Landranger 150 (Worcester & The Malverns) and Pathfinder 997, SP 05/15 (Stratford-upon-Avon (West) & Alcester)

Primrose Hill rises to 350ft (107m) above the Arrow valley between the old market town of Alcester and the riverside village of Wixford. The first part of the walk climbs the hill, passing by Oversley Wood, an attractive remnant of the Forest of Arden, to descend to Wixford; the second part returns to Alcester along the hill's western flanks, following the line of the Roman Ryknild Street. The shorter version omits the detour to Wixford.

Alcester is one of the most appealing small towns in Warwickshire; a varied but harmonious mixture of stone, brick and half-timbered houses dating mainly from the 16th to 18th centuries, with a number of inns and teashops to cater for its visitors. The two most notable buildings in the town centre are the 17th-century Town Hall and the medieval church, with its tall 13th-century tower and surprising 18th-century classical interior.

The walk starts by the Town Hall and church. Pass the east end of the church and keep ahead along the pedestrianised Malt Mill Lane, a picturesque collection of brick and half-timbered cottages, turning right at the end. Soon you turn left along a tarmac path, by the River Arrow, to a road. Continue along the lane opposite to Oversley Green, crossing the river by the confluence of the Alne and Arrow.

Shortly, turn right along Mill Lane **Ⓐ** and, by a group of black-and-white thatched cottages, turn left into Primrose Lane. At the end of the lane cross a bridge

over the Alcester bypass (Heart of England Way sign) and on the other side, ignoring the stile in front, turn left, at a public bridleway sign, down a tarmac fenced track, turning right through a gate at the bottom. Take the uphill track ahead, passing to the left of a bungalow and soon joining another tarmac track. Continue uphill and, just in front of a large house, bear slightly right to go through a gate and along a track which follows the right-hand edge of Oversley Wood, an isolated remnant of the ancient Forest of Arden.

Bear right to reach a junction of tracks **Ⓑ** and here turn right along another very attractive tree-lined track to head gently uphill. In front is a fine view of the east front of Ragley Hall. Later you rejoin the Heart of England Way; keep ahead, below the 19th-century folly of Oversley Castle on the left and passing barns and houses on the right, then continue gently downhill, bearing left at the next bridleway sign. Now omes a fine view ahead across the Avon valley looking towards the Vale of Evesham, with the Cotswolds on the horizon. At a T-junction, turn right along a downhill tarmac track, following it around several bends, passing to the left of Oversley Farm and going through an iron gate to a crossroads of tracks by Wixford church **C**. This small and isolated church is particularly noted for the brasswork dating from the 15th-century on the tomb of Thomas Crewe and his wife.

At this point, those wishing to do only the shorter version of the walk turn right to avoid Wixford and follow the directions after **C** *below.*

For the full walk, keep ahead, passing to the left of the church, along a grassy path to a redundant metal gate. Pass beside it, continue along a wooded path, by a fence on the left, to climb a stile and bear left along a path above the valley. Climb another stile, pass through a small caravan site and go through a gate on to the road, by the bridge over the River Arrow on the right and the Fish Inn on the left.

Turn left along the road through the small village of Wixford, by a number of half-timbered cottages on the right and, just past the last house on the left, bear left to climb a stile **D**. Bear left again to head diagonally across a field, climbing a stile in a hedge on the far side to descend to a sunken lane. Turn left along the lane to return to the crossroads of tracks by Wixford church **C**.

Now keep ahead, at a public bridleway sign, along a track which follows the line of the Roman road of Ryknild (or Icknield) Street, which ran across the Midlands from the Peak District to the Cotswolds. This track, sunken and enclosed at times and variously tree- and hedge-lined, runs in a straight line, eventually bearing right to a gate. Go through, recross the Alcester

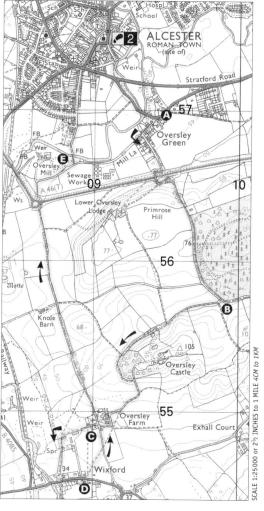

SCALE 1:25 000 or 2½ INCHES to 1 MILE 4CM to 1KM

0	200	400	600	800 METRES	1		
						KILOMETRES	
0	200	400	600 YARDS	½		MILES	

bypass (to the right of an island) and keep ahead to pass through another gate.

Continue, by a hedge on the right, to go through a metal gate on to a tarmac lane and turn right along it for ¼ mile (400km). Near the end of a caravan site on the left, turn left, at a public footpath sign **E** along a tarmac path between fences, cross the River Arrow and keep ahead, with the tower of Alcester church directly in front. Continue along the road into Alcester and, at a crossroads, keep ahead along the main street back to the church and Town Hall.

Kinver Edge

Start	Kinver
Distance	4½ mile (7.2km). Shorter version 2½ miles (4km)
Approximate time	2½ hours (1½ hours for shorter version)
Parking	Kinver
Refreshments	Pubs and cafés at Kinver
Ordnance Survey maps	Landranger 138 (Kidderminster & Wyre Forest) and Pathfinder 933, SO 88/98 (Stourbridge & Kinver)

*With its steep wooded hillsides, extensive footpaths and fine views, the prominent sandstone escarpment of Kinver Edge, now protected by the National Trust and Staffordshire and Hereford and Worcester councils, is very popular with walkers. It is also famed for its rock houses, caves excavated from the sandstone. The full walk has two climbs and two steep descents; the shorter version omits Kinver and starts at point **Ⓐ**, where there are parking facilities.*

The former iron forging village of Kinver lies in the valley of the River Stour which also contains the Staffordshire and Worcestershire Canal, built by Brindley to create a link between the River Severn and the Trent and Mersey Canal. High above the village stands the church, built of the local red sandstone.

Start in the main street in front of the library and turn up Vicarage Drive; soon the lane ends and at a public footpath sign bear right on to an uphill track which curves to the right. At the next public footpath sign, in front of a gate, turn left through a metal gate and walk along a narrow path, between hedges on the right and a fence on the left. The path descends to a lane; turn right along it and take the first left to head uphill. After just under ½ mile (800m), at the top of the hill, turn right through a wooden barrier at a National Trust sign for Kinver Edge **Ⓐ**.

This is the starting point for those doing the shorter version of the walk.

Take the path straight ahead, initially along the right-hand edge of thick woodland. Later the sandy path continues, alongside a wire fence on the left, across an area of gorse, heather, bracken and scattered trees to reach the rim of the escarpment **Ⓑ**. Here a splendid view unfolds, over the steep, thickly wooded slopes of the Edge.

Turn left along the broad track that runs along the top of Kinver Edge and descend slightly to pass through a wooden barrier to a finger-post which indicates the meeting point of three long distance routes: the Staffordshire Way, Worcestershire Way and North Worcestershire Path **Ⓒ**. For the next part of the walk you need to follow the directions closely as there are many paths, tracks and waymarked trails which can make it difficult to keep to a precise route.

By the finger-post turn right to follow a blue-waymarked track downhill through woodland. The track curves to the left and

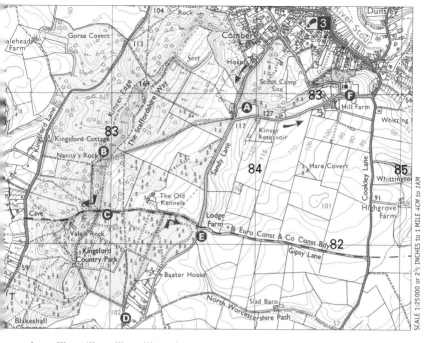

0 200 400 600 800 METRES 1
KILOMETRES
MILES
0 200 400 600 YARDS ½

shortly afterwards, where it curves to the right, keep ahead along a narrower path, following Worcestershire Way signs and turning right at one point, to continue down to the base of the Edge to join a broad track.

Keep ahead to a junction of tracks and turn left to follow a blue waymark, passing to the right of Vale's Rock, one of the area's cave dwellings. Apparently it was occupied until the early 1960s. Continue steadily uphill to a junction of tracks, keep ahead a few yards to the next junction on the brow of the hill, and here turn left to follow a winding uphill path between trees and bracken, climbing steeply to regain the top of the Edge.

Turn left on meeting a track and at a junction of tracks a few yards in front keep straight ahead on the right-hand one. Pass beside a wooden barrier to a T-junction of tracks, turn left and pass beside another barrier to continue along a straight track by the right-hand edge of the woodlands of Kingsford Country Park.

At a gate and wooden barrier, turn left **D** along a blue-waymarked track and at a junction a few yards ahead continue along the right-hand track.

At a T-junction in front of a Country Park information board, turn left for a few yards and then turn right along a track, as far as another T-junction of tracks in front of a wooden fence. Here turn right along the edge of the conifers to emerge on to a lane by a car park **E**. Turn left along the lane for ¹/₂ mile (800m) and take the first turning on the right (Church Road), signposted to Kinver and Bridgnorth **A**.

This is the finishing point for those doing the shorter version of the walk.

Continue as far as Kinver church and turn left **F** along the lane that passes in front of it. The lane bends sharply to the left, heads downhill and then bends sharply to the right. At a footpath sign turn very sharply right along a track which soon bears left and heads downhill in front of houses. By another footpath sign and the wall of a house, turn left down some steps and continue along a downhill path leading directly back to the main street of Kinver. ●

Needwood Forest

Start	At road junction by northern corner of Tomlinson's Corner Wood
Distance	5 miles (8km). Shorter version 3½ miles (5.6km)
Approximate time	2½ hours (1½ hours for shorter version)
Parking	Plenty of wide verges near Tomlinson's Corner Wood
Refreshments	None
Ordnance Survey maps	Landranger 128 (Derby & Burton upon Trent), Pathfinder 851 SK 02/12 (Abbots Bromley)

Detached woodlands, separated by farmland, are all that remain of the once extensive Needwood Forest. This walk, however, captures something of the flavour of the old forest, with some fine wooded stretches and glorious views from the ridge of Forest Banks and Banktop Wood over the Dove valley, looking towards the Peak District and Staffordshire moorlands. The shorter version climbs through woodland to rejoin the main route in Banktop Wood.

Originally a chase and later a royal forest – part of the Duchy of Lancaster – Needwood once covered most of the area of Staffordshire between the rivers Dove, Trent and Blythe and was renowned for its fine oaks and good hunting. Attempts to maintain and replenish the forest during the 17th and 18th centuries failed, and in the 19th century most of the woodland was felled. Nevertheless some splendid remnants survive, even if comparatively small and widely scattered.

From the T-junction by Tomlinson's Corner Wood walk along the road in the Marchington Woodlands and Uttoxeter direction, soon entering the woodlands of Forest Banks. Head downhill and, at a public footpath sign **A**, turn right along a grassy track which keeps below the edge of the wooded cliff to the right. At the next footpath sign ignore a stile on the left and continue along the edge of the wood, following as it curves to the left.

Now the track becomes a narrower path with extensive views to the left across fields and hills to the moorlands on the horizon. Turn left through a gate at a public footpath sign and turn right to keep along the right-hand edge of a field, by a wire fence on the right. Descend to cross a footbridge over a brook, climb a stile and head uphill, continuing along the right-hand edge of a field. In a short while, you leave the edge of the woodland (which veers to the right), keeping ahead, still by a wire fence on the right, towards a farm. Go through a metal gate and bear right along a track, passing to the right of the farm buildings and following the track to a road.

Turn right along the road to ascend Marchington Cliff and, just after the road bends sharply to the right, turn left along a track **B**, again below a wooded cliff.

For the shorter version of the walk bear right uphill, near a house on the left,

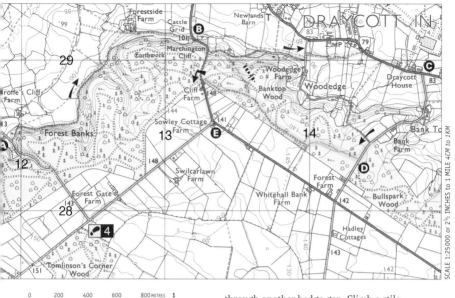

The view from the heights of Forest Banks

looking out for and climbing a distinct
track through the wood to reach a
T-junction of tracks at the top. Here you
turn right to rejoin the main route in
Banktop Wood.

For the full walk keep along the track
as far as a T-junction, turn left for a few
yards, then turn right to climb a stile and
continue along the left-hand edge of a
field, by a hedge on the left. Cross a brook
to continue along the right-hand edge of a
field, go through a hedge gap and keep
along the left-hand edge of a field,
bearing left at the end of it to pass

through another hedge gap. Climb a stile
in front and turn half-left, heading
diagonally across the next field to climb a
stile in the far corner on to a road. Turn
right along it, taking the first turning on
the right (Banktop Road) **Ⓒ**.

Follow this winding lane uphill for
¹/₂ mile (800m), re-entering woodland on
reaching the top. Soon afterwards you
come to a small clearing with forestry
barriers on both sides of the road **Ⓓ**; here
turn right (passing beside one of these
barriers) to follow a clear track through
the very attractive Banktop Wood. It is on
this part of the walk that you can best
appreciate the medieval Needwood Forest,
and there are fine views to the right
through the trees across the Dove valley.
Keep straight ahead along the main track
all the time; this track later curves to the
left and then bears right to continue
through the wood to a road.

Turn left and at the first junction **Ⓔ**
turn right along a lane signposted to Hoar
Cross, following it in a straight line for
just over ¹/₂ mile (800m) back to the
starting point and enjoying sweeping
views all the way across an open
landscape of fields and detached
woodlands that is characteristic of
present-day Needwood.

Marquis Drive
and Castle Ring

Start	Brereton Spurs car park and picnic area
Distance	5 miles (8km)
Approximate time	2½ hours
Parking	Brereton Spurs
Refreshments	None
Ordnance Survey maps	Landranger 128 (Derby & Burton upon Trent) and Explorer 6 (Cannock Chase)

Two commanding viewpoints are the chief focal points of this hilly walk on easy and well-defined tracks amidst the woodland and heathland of Cannock Chase. One of these, Castle Ring, has the distinction of being the highest point in the Chase, at 801ft (244m), and occupies the site of an extensive prehistoric fort.

Brereton Spurs car park and picnic area occupy an open and elevated position from which there are fine views over both the Trent valley and Cannock Chase.

Turn left out of the car park and walk along the road, descending gently to reach a junction. A few yards before the junction turn sharply to the right along a broad downhill track **A**; this is the Marquis Drive, named after a 19th-century Marquis of Anglesey who had it

Looking over Cannock Chase from Castle Ring

constructed as a carriage drive. The track undulates through an area of conifer forest edged with broadleaved trees, with fine wooded views, curving to the left and then to the right, and passing to the right of a pool to continue downhill, by a stream on the right, to a road.

Just before reaching the road, turn sharp left (passing beside a forestry barrier) along an uphill track **B**. Bear right at a fork and at a junction of four tracks a few yards ahead, keep straight ahead along an uphill track between conifers. This track later levels out to arrive at a crossroads of tracks on the edge of a golf course. Continue across the course, taking care to avoid low-flying golf balls, to another crossroads of tracks and keep ahead again, descending to a road. Turn left and, opposite the entrance to the golf club

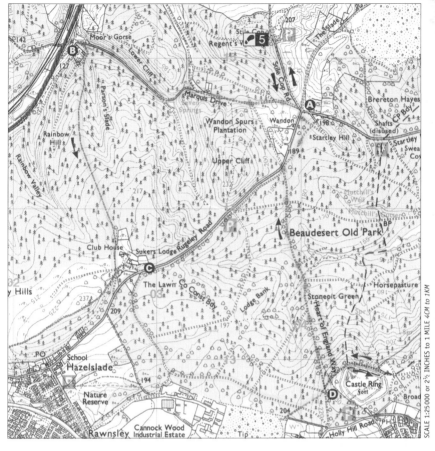

SCALE 1:25000 or 2½ INCHES to 1 MILE 4CM to 1KM

```
0        200    400    600    800 METRES  1
                                           KILOMETRES
                                           MILES
0        200    400    600 YARDS      ½
```

car park **C**, turn right, passing beside a forestry barrier, along a track that continues between more tall conifers. This area was once part of Beaudesert Old Park but the hall, home of the Pagets (marquises of Anglesey) who owned a great deal of Cannock Chase, was demolished in 1932.

After a while the track bears left and then continues in more or less a straight line, later passing to the left of a pool beyond which is the partially landscaped tip of a former colliery – a reminder of the chase's industrial history. (Coal mines became established around its southern fringes in the 19th century.) Continue gently uphill to a crossroads, here bearing left along an uphill path to cross a track

and, a few yards ahead, reach a second and broader track **D**.

A short detour ahead brings you to Castle Ring, a large Iron Age fort whose well-preserved ramparts and ditches offer extensive views of the Trent valley.

The route continues by turning left (or right if you have made the detour) along this broad track, which heads downhill. Keep ahead at a junction and, where the track later forks, take the left-hand track, cross a small stream, keep ahead to cross another and continue uphill in a straight line to reach a road. Just before the road turn right, at a Heart of England Way sign, along a track. At the next such sign, turn left and pass beside a barrier on to the road. Turn right for a few yards to a junction **A**, where you rejoin the outward route, bearing left along Stile Cop Road to retrace your steps to the starting point. ●

Henley-in-Arden and Preston Bagot

Henley-in-Arden and Preston Bagot

Start	Henley-in-Arden
Distance	5 miles (8km)
Approximate time	2½ hours
Parking	Henley-in-Arden
Refreshments	Pubs and cafés at Henley-in-Arden, pub at Preston Bagot
Ordnance Survey maps	Landranger 151 (Stratford-upon-Avon) and Pathfinder 975, SP 06/16 (Redditch & Henley-in-Arden)

Although a modest walk in the gentle rolling countryside of Arden, the first part is quite hilly in places. From Henley-in-Arden the route heads across fields, climbing to the hilltop church of Preston Bagot. Then it descends to the Stratford-upon-Avon Canal and the rest of the walk is a pleasant and easy stroll, first along the banks of the canal and later by the River Alne.

Henley-in-Arden's attractive and distinctive ¾-mile-long (1.25km) High Street comprises a mixture of brick and half-timbered buildings. Roughly half-way along are the timber-framed Guildhall and the church, both dating from the 15th century.

The walk starts by the church; turn down Beaudesert Lane and cross the River Alne to reach the 12th-century Beaudesert church. It is surprising to find two churches so close together, but Beaudesert was originally a separate settlement at the foot of the castle of the de Montforts.

Just past the church, go through a metal kissing-gate, at public footpath and Heart of England Way signs, to head uphill across the complex of earthworks that is all that remains of the great castle of the de Montforts. Keep in a straight line along an obvious path, finally heading up to a pair of stiles.

Climb the right-hand stile and walk along the right-hand edge of a field, by a hedge and wire fence on the right. Where you see a stile on the right, turn half-left and continue across the field towards a public footpath sign and stile. Climb the stile on to a lane, bear left, following the lane around a right-hand bend, and where it bends to the left **A**, keep ahead through a metal gate and along a tarmac drive. Climb a stile to the right of the next gate and continue along a narrow hedge-lined path, passing to the right of a house and continuing by a metal fence on the left. Later keep along the left-hand edge of a field, climb a stile, continue straight across the next field and about half-way across it, turn left and head across to the far side, making for a stile in a hedge. Climb it and continue along the left-hand edge of a series of fields, by a hedge on the left all the while, climbing a succession of stiles. When you see farm buildings in front, head across the middle of a field, aiming for a waymarked stile to the right of them.

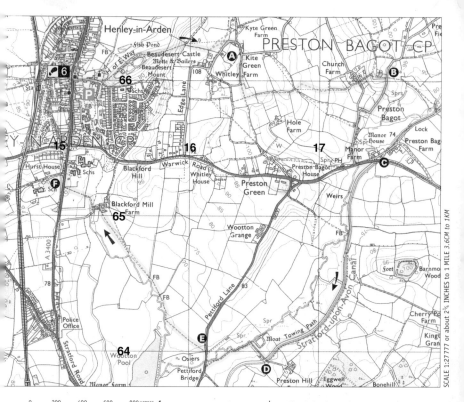

SCALE 1:27777 or about 2¼ INCHES to 1 MILE 3.6CM to 1KM

Climb the stile, keep ahead to climb two more and finally go through a gate on to a lane just to the right of a black-and-white cottage. Cross the lane and take the uphill path ahead, curving to the right to go through a kissing-gate and bearing left to pass to the right of Preston Bagot church, a small isolated church with a bell-turret.

Go through a metal kissing-gate on to a narrow lane **B** and turn right; the lane bends first to the right and then to the left to reach a T-junction. Turn left for ¼ mile (400m) to a road – there is a pub just to the right – and turn left again in the direction of Claverdon and Warwick. Cross a stream and continue to the canal bridge – on the left is the half-timbered, 16th-century Preston Bagot Manor House.

Just before the bridge, turn right to the canal bank **C**, do not cross the bridge in front, but turn right again to go through a gate. Now follow the canal towpath for the next 1¼ miles (2km), to the second bridge **D**. Here turn right along a tarmac track which bends to the left, to reach a road. Turn right, cross a bridge and after 50 yds (46m) turn left over a stile **E**.

Bear right and head diagonally across a large field to a stile in the far corner, where you meet the River Alne. Climb the stile and continue by the meandering river. On approaching Blackford Mill Farm, the path turns first right and then left to continue up to a metal gate.

Go through, turn left and immediately go through another metal gate to pass in front of the buildings. Follow a public footpath sign to the right, pass through a gate, then cross a footbridge over the river and keep along the narrow path ahead, by a wire fence and later a wooden fence on the right, to a stile. Climb this and then continue in a straight line across a school playing-field to climb another stile at the far end on to the main road **F**. Turn right and then follow the road back into Henley-in-Arden.

●

Ellesmere Lakes

Start	Ellesmere
Distance	6½ miles (10.5km)
Approximate time	3½ hours
Parking	Canal Wharf at Ellesmere
Refreshments	Pubs and cafés at Ellesmere
Ordnance Survey maps	Landranger 126 (Shrewsbury), Pathfinders 827, SJ 23/33 (Chirk & Ellesmere) and 828 SJ 43/53 (Ellesmere (East) & Prees)

The 'Shropshire Lake District' around Ellesmere, a collection of shallow, tree-fringed meres, is a southern continuation of the mere country of Cheshire. Much of the land surrounding the meres is private, but by combining rights of way with sections of road, canal towpaths and waymarked trails, a very satisfying and enjoyable walk can be devised around this highly distinctive area.

Ellesmere is dominated by its restored, mainly 15th-century cruciform church whose imposing tower overlooks The Mere, largest of the ten meres in the area. All these meres were formed as a result of glacial action in the last Ice Age; meltwaters spread huge amounts of rocks and soils over the lowlands of Cheshire and north Shropshire, scooping out hollows and shallow depressions which filled with water. Unlike most lakes, these have no streams flowing in or out.

The meres are one of Ellesmere's twin attractions; the other is its canal heritage, and the warehouse and crane at the Canal Wharf, where the walk begins, are reminders that Ellesmere was once an important trading town on the Llangollen Canal, built by Telford to link North Wales with the Mersey.

Begin by taking the towpath on the right bank of the canal, turn left over the first bridge, by the junction of the short Ellesmere spur and the main canal **A**, and turn right to continue along the left bank. From here to Cole Mere is a most

attractive stretch of the canal; remote, peaceful and mainly tree-lined. Pass under a bridge, then through a tunnel to reach and follow the edge of Blake Mere.

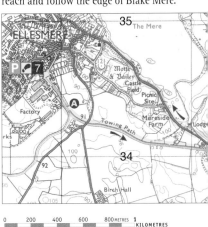

Shortly after passing under another bridge, you see a thatched half-timbered house on the right, and beyond that a view of Cole Mere.

At the next bridge, leave the canal and turn right over the bridge **B**. Continue down a lane for a few yards and turn left through a gate into Yell Wood, here entering Colemere Country Park. Follow a clear and broad track through the wood – there are some fine old beech trees and pleasant views through the trees on the right across the mere. After a while this track heads up to the canal bank by a bridge. Do not cross the bridge, but continue briefly along the side of the canal before turning right, going down some steps and then following a broad and clearly defined path to a gate on the edge of the wood.

Continue across the flat meadowland ahead, keeping by the edge of the mere, climb a stile (or go through the gate to the left of it) and turn right along the right-hand edge of the meadow, by a high wire fence on the right, to join a track **C**. Keep ahead along the track, go through a gate and continue through Boathouse Wood. This is a lovely part of the walk, with attractive views to the right across Cole Mere. Ignoring a gate and footpath sign on the right, keep ahead for about another 50 yds (46m) to go through a kissing-gate on to a lane and follow the lane back up to the canal bridge **B**.

Cross the bridge and, at a public footpath sign, turn left along a path that heads uphill and continues along the left-hand edge of a field, following the field edge as it curves right and keeping by a hedge on the left. Soon there is a fine view ahead of Newton Mere. The path widens into a track, bears right and continues between hedges to a lane opposite Newton Mere **D**.

Turn left along the lane to a junction and left again along the road signposted to Ellesmere (note: this is a busy road and extreme care should be taken). Follow this road for $^1/_2$ mile (800m) – there is a particularly fine view to the left over the small Kettle Mere to Blake Mere beyond – and just where the road bends sharply to the left, climb a yellow-waymarked stile on the right **E**. Head over the hill, bearing right and descending to climb another stile on to a road. Turn right towards Ellesmere along the western edge of The Mere, passing The Meres Visitor Centre, which describes how the meres were formed and the wildlife to be found around them. In the town, pass to the right of the church and follow the signs to the Canal Wharf.

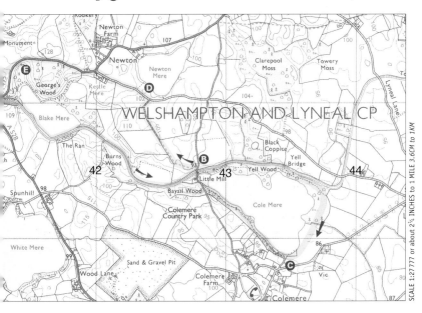

Sutton Park

Start	Sutton Park Visitor Centre – just beyond Town Gate ½ mile (800m) to the west of Sutton Coldfield town centre
Distance	6½ miles (10.5km)
Approximate time	3½ hours
Parking	Car park near visitor centre
Refreshments	Several restaurants, cafés and kiosks in Sutton Park
Ordnance Survey maps	Landranger 139 (Birmingham) and Pathfinder 913, SP 09/19 (Sutton Coldfield & Walsall)

Sutton Park is a miraculous survival; a genuine oasis of wild country, a remnant of the extensive forest and heathland that once covered much of the Midlands, entirely within the boundaries of Birmingham and encircled by roads and residential suburbs. The first part of the walk is predominantly across open heathland, the second part is mainly through thick woodland, and the various pools that are dotted around the park act as focal points – highly attractive scenic features. The large number of paths and tracks can make it difficult in places to keep to a precise route – especially in the northern part of the walk through the woodlands of Gum Slade – but given the relatively small size of the park – about 2400 acres – the park roads and pools, which are useful landmarks, and its popularity with walkers, it is impossible to remain lost for long even if you do happen to stray from the route.

For the survival of Sutton Park virtually unchanged through the centuries we are mainly indebted to Bishop Vesey, a 16th-century bishop of Exeter and native of Sutton Coldfield. After receiving the lands of Sutton Chase from Henry VIII, he presented them to the people of the town in perpetuity and, despite commercial and residential pressures, encroachment has on the whole been successfully resisted, apart from the building of a railway across the park in the late 19th century.

From the car park by the Town Gate and visitor centre, head across the grass to the visitor centre and continue past it, bearing left to stay beside the park road. Keep to the right where the road forks and follow it to a T-junction, where you turn left down towards Powell's Pool.

Just before the pool **A** turn right to follow a path across grass, by the edge of trees on the right. At the end of the grassy expanse, turn left in the direction of the pool and, about 100 yds (91m) before reaching it, turn right through a narrow belt of trees to emerge on to a track. Follow the track along the left-hand edge of open heathland, by trees and the

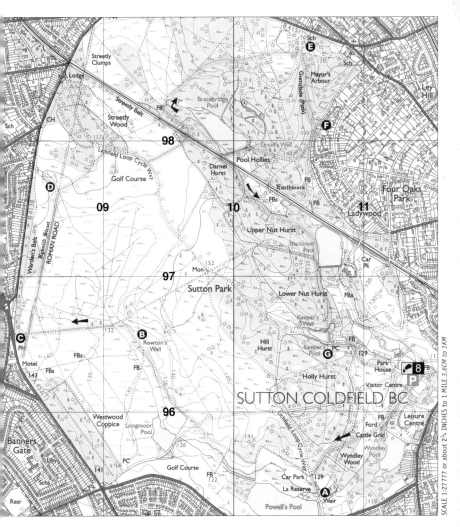

Streetly
Clumps

Lodge

Streetly Belt

Streetly
Wood

FB

Bracebridge
Pool

98

Lichfield Loop Cycle Way

Golf Course

Darnel
Hurst

Pool Hollies

Druid's Well

Sch

E

Mayor's
Arbour

Gumslade (Path)

F

Ley
Hill

Sch

Four Oaks
Park

D

09

Warden's Belt

ROMAN ROAD

Icknield Street

132

10

Earthwork

FBs

Upper Nut Hurst

Blackroot
Pool

11
Ladywood

Car
Pk

97

Mon

152

Sutton Park

Lower Nut Hurst

FBs

Keeper's
Well

SCALE 1:27 777 or about 2¾ INCHES to 1 MILE 3.6CM to 1KM

C

PH

Motel

143

FBs

FBs

B

Rowton's
Well

FB

Hill
Hurst

Keeper's
Pool

G

PC

129

FB

B

Park
House

Visitor Centre

8

P

96

Westwood
Coppice

Longmoor
Pool

SUTTON COLDFIELD BC

Lichfield Loop Cycle Way

FB

Ford

Cattle Grid

Leisure
Centre

Wyndley
Pool

Banners
Gate

Luby

Schs

PC

141

126

Golf Course

FB
122

Wyndley
Wood

Car Park

129

La Reserve

A

Weir

118

Resr

Powell's Pool

| 0 | 200 | 400 | 600 | 800 METRES | 1 |
| 0 | 200 | 400 | 600 YARDS | ½ | KILOMETRES / MILES |

boundary fence of a golf course on the left, to a road. To the left is Longmoor Pool. Cross the road and keep ahead, passing to the left of a circle of trees – Queen's Coppice, planted to commemorate Elizabeth II's coronation in 1953. Ahead there are grand views across the rough grassland, gorse, heather and woodlands of Rowton Heath to a low ridge. At a junction of tracks **B**, turn left and soon bear left again on joining a broad straight track. Follow this track (Lord Donegal's Ride) over a brook and on towards the park boundary.

About 150 yds (137m) before reaching the gate and road on the edge of the park **C**, turn right on to another straight track which follows the line of the Roman road of Ryknild (or Icknield) Street. This is a route which ran north–south across the Midlands from the Peak District to the Cotswolds. The track soon heads across a golf course and, after crossing a brook **D**, bear slightly right to continue walking across the golf course, passing through a superb oak glade and on to a road. Turn right and, on emerging from the trees, turn left along a broad track. Pass beside a gate to enter woodland, then cross a railway bridge and now the track initially bends to the left and later curves to the

Ancient oaks in Gum Slade, Sutton Park

right to pass across the end of Little
Bracebridge Pool.

It is between here and Bracebridge Pool
that careful attention should be paid to
the route directions. At the first fork keep
ahead to a second fork a few yards in
front and here bear right to continue
across a partly felled area to a crossroads
of tracks. Bear left and head gently uphill
by some fine silver birches, keep ahead at
the next crossroads (there is a bench by a
tree here) and continue along the left-
hand edge of woodland.

On entering the woodland, turn half-
left (not fully left) along a track – the
television transmitter straight ahead acts
as a useful landmark. This track bears
slightly left to a T-junction **E**. Turn right
and after a few yards you reach a small
grassy clearing; here turn right again on
to an initially narrower path which soon
becomes a well-defined track that winds
through the splendid ancient oak
woodland of Gum Slade, a superb part of
the walk. On reaching a park road **F** turn

right, turn right again at a junction, walk
through a car park and continue along the
track towards Bracebridge Pool.

Just before the track reaches the pool,
turn left down some steps and walk along
the edge of it. Bracebridge Pool is often
regarded as the most beautiful expanse of
water in the park. It was made for Sir
Ralph Bracebridge, who obtained the lease
on the manor and chase of Sutton
Coldfield from the Earl of Warwick in
1419, in order to ensure a plentiful supply
of fish. At the end of the pool recross the
railway and bear left along a track. The
rest of the walk is along clear and easy
tracks through most attractive woodland.

Go through a kissing-gate, keep ahead
to pass by a redundant stile and continue,
soon arriving at Blackroot Pool. Keep
along the edge of the pool and continue
through more woodland to pass along the
end of the smaller Keeper's Pool, formed
in the 15th century (by damming a small
stream) as a source of fish for the park
keeper. At the end of the pool **G** turn left,
pass beside a gate and follow the road
ahead back to the start.

Tanworth-in-Arden

Start	Tanworth-in-Arden
Distance	6½ miles (10.5km)
Approximate time	3½ hours
Parking	Roadside parking by the Green at Tanworth-in-Arden
Refreshments	Pub at Tanworth-in-Arden
Ordnance Survey maps	Landranger 139 (Birmingham), Pathfinders 954, SP 07/17 (Solihull & Alvechurch) and 975, SP 06/16 (Redditch & Henley-in-Arden)

Shakespeare's Forest of Arden, a large tract of woodland, heath and pasture that once stretched over most of Warwickshire north of the River Avon, has virtually disappeared, but this undemanding and highly enjoyable walk in the heart of the former forest around Tanworth-in-Arden reveals a still well-wooded countryside. Despite being close to the M42 and scarcely more than 12 miles (19km) from the centre of Birmingham, the walk also reveals a surprisingly peaceful, unchanged rural landscape. There are a few muddy sections and two small streams to ford, though the latter should present no problems, except possibly after prolonged rain.

The hilltop village of Tanworth-in-Arden is a most attractive mixture of brick and halftimbered cottages, with the traditional grouping of inn and church around a triangular green. The tower and spire of the 14th-century church dominate the surrounding landscape and are in sight for much of the walk.

Begin at the Green by facing the church and walking to the left of it down a lane of pleasant old cottages. Cross a lane on the right (signposted to Danzey Green) and, at a public footpath sign and 'Private Road to Leasowes Farm' notice, turn right along a straight, undulating, tarmac, tree-lined drive **Ⓐ**. Follow this drive, formerly the drive leading to Umberslade Hall, for 1¼ miles (2km). Soon after passing under a railway bridge the drive turns right, but you continue ahead along a track now lined more informally with trees and with views on both sides. Later the façade of Umberslade Hall is seen ahead.

Eventually climb a stile on to a lane **Ⓑ** and turn right along it for just over ½ mile (800m), ignoring the first stile and public footpath sign on the right but turning right over the second stile **Ⓒ**. Walk along a track, pass through a wide hedge gap and continue downhill across a field, by a hedge and line of trees on the left, veering right near the bottom end of the field to climb a stile. Now continue along the right-hand edge of a field, by a wire fence and hedge on the right, looking out for a public footpath sign, where you turn left and head straight across the middle of the field to a stile. Climb it, continue, passing through a hedge gap, and keep along a now obvious path that

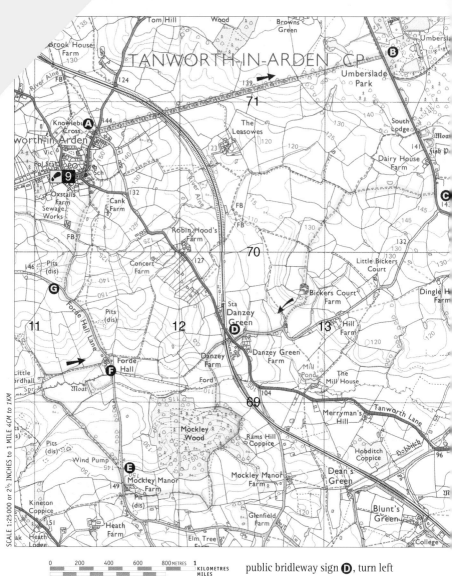

0	200	400	600	800 METRES	1
					KILOMETRES
					MILES
0	200	400	600 YARDS	½	

heads gently uphill across the next field to a metal gate. Go through, bear slightly left (by a pool on the left) to keep along the left-hand side of a field, go through another gate and continue to a farm. In front of the farm turn left over a stile, turn right along a track, passing to the left of the house, and continue along a track which curves to the right and heads downhill to a lane.

Turn right to head up to a T-junction, turn right again for a few yards and, at a public bridleway sign **D**, turn left through a metal gate and over a railway bridge. Keep ahead to go through another metal gate and turn left along a track, by a hedge on the left and a wire fence on the right, that heads gently downhill to ford a stream. Go through a metal gate, climb over the stile in front, and continue across a field to climb another stile into Mockley Wood.

Bear left to follow a path along the edge of the wood between wire fences. The path curves to the right, heading uphill all the while alongside this lovely, predominantly birch wood – an impressive reminder of the old Forest of Arden – to reach a stile. Climb it and keep ahead along a broad track which curves left and heads downhill, between high wire fences. In front of a formidable-looking metal gate, bear right to go through a much smaller gate and keep along the right-hand edge of a field, following the field edge round to the right to climb a stile in the far corner. Keep ahead to go through a metal gate and continue along the right-hand, top edge of a sloping field, by a fence and hedge on the right, to another stile. Climb this stile and then continue by a fine group of trees on the right, passing to the left of a large house (Mockley Manor) and heading down to climb over another stile to reach a lane.

Turn right and, just where the lane starts to descend **E**, bear left along a track to climb a waymarked stile. Keep ahead along a tree-lined path – sunken and possibly muddy and overgrown at the start, but it improves – to go through a metal gate. Continue, curving gradually to the right, to ford a stream in front of a house and climb a stile on the other side. Keep ahead, passing to the right of the house, to a field corner; here do not climb the stile in front, but turn right along the edge of the field, by a wire fence on the left. Go through a metal gate and continue along a track, passing between farm buildings and to the left of a house, on to a lane **F**.

Turn left uphill for nearly ¹/₂ mile (800m) cross a stile and, just before the lane curves gently to the left, turn right over another stile

by a yellow waymarker **G** and walk across a field, by trees and a wire fence on the right. The buildings of Tanworth can be seen on the ridge ahead, clustered around the church. Head downhill to climb a stile and bear slightly left across the next field in the direction of the church. Near the far end, follow a brook around a left-hand bend, then cross it and climb a stile. Now follow a straight and well-defined path uphill across a field, climb a stile and turn left towards a bungalow. Climb another stile and continue along a narrow path between bushes on the left and the garden fence of the bungalow on the right to a lane. Turn left back to the start. ●

Medieval church overlooking the village green at Tanworth-in-Arden

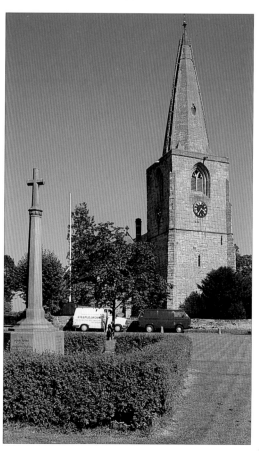

Stokesay Castle and View Wood

Start	Stokesay Castle
Distance	5½ miles (8.9km)
Approximate time	3 hours
Parking	Stokesay Castle – alternatively use lay-by on A49 just to north of turning to Stokesay Castle
Refreshments	None
Ordnance Survey maps	Landranger 137 (Ludlow & Wenlock Edge), Pathfinders 931, SO 48/58 (Craven Arms) and 951, SO 47/57 (Ludlow)

Only the fortified manor house of Stokesay Castle indicates that this now peaceful countryside near the Welsh border was once a bloody battleground between Saxon and Celt. There are three separate but modest climbs on this walk, which is well-waymarked throughout, passing through some lovely wooded stretches and providing outstanding views over a largely unchanged landscape.

There could hardly be a more romantic looking grouping than that of the medieval manor house with its half-timbered gatehouse and adjacent church at Stokesay, especially when viewed from across the pool to the west. Its setting amidst the well-wooded hills of the Onny valley adds to the overall attractiveness of the scene. Despite its name, Stokesay Castle was not a castle but a manor house, built by a local wool merchant, Lawrence of Ludlow, who purchased the manor in 1280. Although not solid enough to offer any serious resistance, the fortifications indicate that this was still a troubled and wartorn area at the time. The church was originally built in the 12th century as a chapel to the castle, but was mostly rebuilt in the Cromwellian era – a period more usually associated with the destruction of churches.

Start at the castle and walk along the lane, passing to the right of the church and castle and to the left of the pool, continuing along a track and bearing right to cross the railway line. Turn left along a stony track to climb a stile **A** and turn right uphill along a field edge, by a hedge on the right. Climb another stile, cross a track and continue uphill along a tree and hedge-lined track. At a footpath sign keep ahead through Stoke Wood – with a fine view from here to the left over the Onny valley – passing over the brow, and continue along the track to a lane. Turn left and after 50 yds (46m) turn right, at a public footpath sign, over a stile **B**. Keep along the left-hand edge of a field, by a hedge and wire fence on the left, climb a stile, head down steps to turn left over another stile a few yards ahead and continue to a lane **C**.

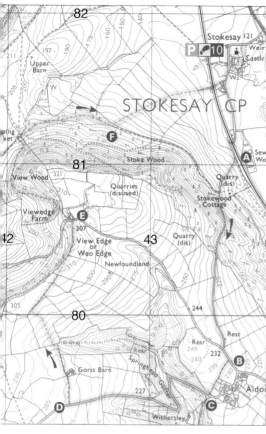

Climb a stile on to a lane opposite a house **E**, turn left and, after a few yards, right along a grassy path to pass behind the house. At this point there is a superb view to the left, looking westwards towards Clun Forest and the Welsh hills. Climb a stile to enter View Wood and follow a well-waymarked path downhill through this most attractive woodland, continuing along the left-hand edge of it and later joining a track to re-enter it. Where the track emerges from the wood, turn right along the top edge of a sloping meadow, keeping by the edge of the wood on the right, to climb a stile and continue along the edge of the wood, now by a wire fence on the right.

At a waymarked post, turn left down to a track, passing to the left of a house, and turn right by the side of the house. Climb the right-hand stile in front to enter a conifer plantation and follow a path between the trees. At the point where the path comes close to the plantation's edge, look out for and climb a stile about 20 yds (18m) to the left of the path **F**.

Bear slightly right across a field and for the rest of the walk there is the grand view of castle and church side by side, pool in front and wooded hills beyond. Keep in the direction of the castle all the while, passing through several fields and over a series of stiles, finally going through a metal gate and along a broad tree-lined track to recross the railway line. Continue along a track, passing between the pool on the left and a barn on the right, go through a gate and turn left to retrace your steps to the start. ●

Turn right along this quiet and narrow lane for ¾ mile (1.25km) – at first downhill, sharp left and over a ford, then uphill and sharp right, continuing as far as a public footpath sign **D**. Here turn right along a track, passing to the left of a house, go through a fence gap ahead and continue along a broad green track, between wire fences, heading downhill and bearing left to a gate. Go through and now walk uphill across the middle of a field, climb a stile and turn right along the right-hand edge of a field, by a wire fence and trees on the right, to another stile. Climb that, keep ahead to climb another and continue, by the edge of woodland and a wire fence on the left. From this open and elevated position there are fine and extensive views all around.

Churnet Valley and Alton

Start	Oakamoor
Distance	6 miles (9.7km)
Approximate time	3 hours
Parking	Car park and picnic site at Oakamoor
Refreshments	Pubs at Oakamoor, café between Oakamoor and Alton, pubs and cafés at Alton
Ordnance Survey maps	Landranger 128 (Derby & Burton upon Trent) and Pathfinder 810, SK 04/14 (Ashbourne & The Churnet Valley)

The steep-sided slopes of the Churnet valley provide fine walking and splendid views amidst a hilly and well-wooded landscape that has been likened to that of Switzerland. Despite its proximity to the Potteries and in particular to the hugely popular Alton Towers, this is a very peaceful and secluded walk. The first half takes an up-and-down course along the south side of the valley to just beyond Alton village; the return, along the north side, is an easy ramble that follows the track of a disused railway.

The car park and picnic site at Oakamoor occupy the site of what was first a tinplate and later a copper-wire works and a few remains are visible; evidence of the former industrial activity in this area. Leave the car park and turn left along a lane through the steep-sided and well-wooded valley with the river on the left, bearing left uphill at a junction. Just after the lane bears left (in front of a high embankment wall on the right), turn right on to a path Ⓐ that heads steeply uphill through woodland, and, near the top, bear right to reach a wall and gate on the edge of the woods about 50 yds (46m) to the right of a house.

Go through the gate and bear right along a broad, grassy, walled track – the wall on the left is somewhat incomplete. Cross another track, go through a gate ahead and a few yards further on turn left

at a footpath sign to join the Staffordshire Way. Keep ahead all the while along a downhill wooded track which passes to the left of a pool, later passes the remains of a smelting mill and continues through the Forestry Commission woodlands of Dimmings Dale to reach a building that was at one time a hunting lodge of the earls of Shrewsbury (former owners of Alton Towers) but is now the Ramblers Retreat Café.

At a public footpath sign to Rakes Dale and Alton Ⓑ turn right, not on to the tarmac lane but along the path parallel to and just above it on the right. This is a most attractive part of the walk, through the wooded valley with the river below. The path climbs steadily between embankments to join a track and you continue along it. Over to the left are the battlements of a Gothic lodge of Alton

0	200	400	600	800 METRES	1

KILOMETRES
MILES

0	200	400	600 YARDS	½

Towers and in front, between the trees, can be seen the towers and turrets of the 19th-century Alton Castle, both of which bestow upon this part of Staffordshire a skyline more reminiscent of the Rhineland or Bavaria.

Keep ahead at a junction, now heading gently downhill to rejoin the lane at a bend. Walk along the lane for a few yards and, where it bends to the left, continue on an uphill wooded path, at a National Trust sign to Toothill Wood and a public footpath sign to Alton, high up along the side of the valley. After bearing right head more steeply uphill, passing to the left of a large rock, climb a stile and continue, passing through a metal gate on to a walled track. A few yards' detour to the left brings you to the superb vantage point of Toothill Rock, overlooking the Churnet valley, Alton village and the Staffordshire moorlands beyond. The main route turns right for a few yards, as far as a Staffordshire Way sign, and then turns left along another walled track directly towards the village. Follow this winding track to come out on to a road by the Royal Oak **C**.

Keep straight ahead, passing to the left of a circular building that was built in 1819 as the village lock-up, to a T-junction. Here bear left and, where the main road curves to the left downhill, continue along High Street, passing to the right of Alton's restored medieval church, which still retains some Norman work. Beyond the church is the 19th-century

Alton Castle, with a few remains in its grounds of the walls of the Norman castle on whose site it stands. The castle, like Alton Towers across the valley, was the creation of the earls of Shrewsbury and is now used as a school and hospital.

Continue through the village to where the tarmac road ends at a farm, and here first bear left and then right along a track, between farm buildings on the left and a wall on the right. At the end of the farm buildings go through a metal gate, keep ahead a few yards to climb a stone stile and immediately turn left over a wooden stile **D**. Head across a field, making for and then keeping by a wall on the left; from here some of the amusement rides of Alton Towers can be seen above the steep wooded slopes opposite. Look out for a stile in the wall, turn left over it and follow a path steeply downhill through woodland, winding between rocks and trees, to reach a track. Here climb another stile and continue downhill to join the River Churnet, following it as far as a footbridge.

Turn left over the bridge, keep ahead to go through a kissing-gate **E** and then turn left along the track of the disused Old Churnet Railway, now a Staffordshire County Council permissive path, which you follow for nearly $2\frac{1}{2}$ miles (4km) back to Oakamoor. This is a lovely stretch of the walk; keeping close to the river, between wooded slopes and with a fine view to the left of the romantic-looking outlines of Alton Castle perched high above the valley. Pass under a road-bridge just by Alton's former station, keep ahead to pass under a second bridge and continue, finally crossing the river and turning right to return to the car park and picnic site.

Alton's 19th-century castle gives a touch of Bavaria or the Rhineland to the area

Lickey Hills

Start	Lickey Hills Visitor Centre, ¼ mile (400m) east of Lickey church off B4096
Distance	5½ miles (8.9km)
Approximate time	3 hours
Parking	Lickey Hills Visitor Centre
Refreshments	Café at visitor centre, pub at Barnt Green, restaurant and café at Rose and Crown near point **E**
Ordnance Survey maps	Landranger 139 (Birmingham), Pathfinders 953, SO 87/97 (Kidderminster & Bromsgrove) and 954, SP 07/17 (Solihull & Alvechurch)

Birmingham's traditional weekend and Bank Holiday playground, the Lickey Hills are a compact range of well-wooded slopes that provide fine walking and grand views on the southern edge of the city. For most of this walk the proximity of the city is surprisingly unnoticeable, but from the 987ft (301m) summit of Beacon Hill, the highest point on the Lickeys, a splendid panorama offers great contrasts: looking directly over Birmingham in one direction, but also extending in a sweeping arc across the rural heart of England to the distant Cotswold, Malvern and Shropshire hills.

Elihu Burritt, American consul in Birmingham in the 1860s and a great walker, wrote: 'there are no hills more grateful and delightful for airing one's body and soul than the Lickey cluster'. From 1887 onwards the hills were acquired as a public recreation area for the people of Birmingham, partly through the generosity of the Cadbury family and partly through purchase from the Earl of Plymouth.

From the front of the visitor centre head downhill across a picnic area to pick up a path on the left. Continue into woodland and, on joining a track, keep ahead through Pinfields Wood. Head gently downhill, keeping on the main track all the while, passing to the right of a wooden shelter and then bearing right at

the bottom of the hill to continue through the woods. Shortly after passing to the left of another wooden shelter, you reach a lane. Turn left for a few yards, then right, go up four steps and continue along a tree-lined track to come out on to a road opposite Barnt Green station **A**.

Turn left along the road and, at a T-junction, turn right along Bittell Road. Pass under the railway bridge and shortly turn left along Margesson Drive **B**. At the end of the drive keep ahead through a sports club car park (there is a half-hidden public footpath sign to Bittell Farm Road), staying on the right of a brick building and, at the end of this building, follow a path to the left and then turn right over a stile. Continue along the left-hand edge of a field and, where the hedge on the left

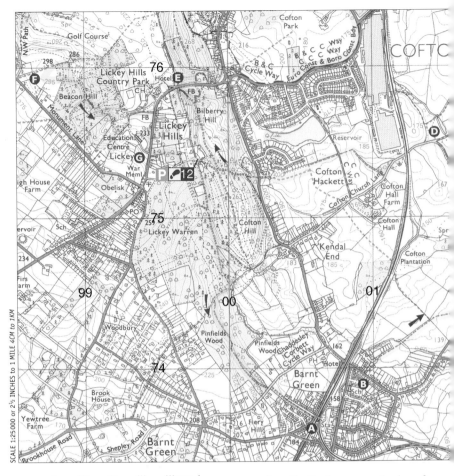

| 0 | 200 | 400 | 600 | 800 METRES | 1 |
| KILOMETRES |
| MILES |
| 0 | 200 | 400 | 600 YARDS | ½ |

finishes, keep ahead to cross a brook, go through a hedge gap and walk along the left-hand edge of the next field to a stile. Climb this and bear right diagonally across the next field to climb over a stile on to a road.

Keep ahead along the road, with reservoirs on both sides, walking gently uphill and, just past a slight left-hand bend, turn left over a stile **C** at a public footpath sign to Upper Bittell Reservoir. Continue along the right-hand edge of a field, between a hedge on the right and a wire fence on the left – with a fine view of the Lickeys on the left. The curving field path heads gently up to a stile; climb it and keep ahead, descending to climb

another stile. Continue across the dam of Upper Bittell Reservoir and, in front of a metal gate, turn left and head down to a stile. Climb this, turn right (public bridleway sign) along a track and follow it to a lane **D**.

Turn left along the lane and, soon after passing under a railway bridge, you come to Cofton Hackett church on the left. This medieval church was heavily restored by the Victorians, but has a timber porch and bell-turret dating from the 15th century. Continue past the church and, at a public footpath sign to Barnt Green Road, turn right over a stile and walk gently uphill along the right-hand edge of a field, by woodland on the right. Turn left at a North Worcestershire Path sign, continue across a field up to a stile, climb it and cross a track to climb another stile. Keep

along the right-hand edge of a field, by a wire fence and later garden fences on the right, climb a stile and follow a tarmac path between fences up to another stile and then on to a road.

Cross over and, at a public footpath sign, take the uphill path opposite through Cofton Woods, turning right at the top of steps, by a North Worcestershire Path sign, along a track which curves to the left and continues uphill. At the top – a few yards ahead, across an open area, is the visitor centre car park – turn sharp right along a track which gives fine views to the right over Birmingham as it continues over Bilberry Hill. Just by a group of rocks (the 'Lickey Rocks') there is a superb view to the left of Beacon Hill. From here the track descends steeply via the 'Hundred Steps' to a road **E**.

Cross this road and turn left to follow North Worcestershire Path waymarks across an ornamental garden area, passing to the right of the Rose and Crown inn and continuing through a car park. Keeping to the right of a building in front (golf shop and café) follow an uphill path alongside the golf course on the right. Climb some steps and turn right, still keeping along the edge of the golf course. The path soon enters trees and, at a convergence of paths, follow a North

Worcestershire Path sign to the left, turn right after a few yards and shortly afterwards turn left to climb steps. Continue uphill to emerge on to the grassy plateau that crowns the summit of Beacon Hill and, shortly after passing a triangulation pillar, bear left off the path and head across the grass to a castellated structure at the summit **F** which houses a toposcope pointing out the places to be seen from this magnificent viewpoint.

At the toposcope, turn left across the grass, keeping by the edge of trees on the left and, at the end of the trees, turn left again to continue along a path by the right-hand edge of woodland. On meeting a track, turn right and keep along it in a straight line all the while, passing several junctions, to descend a long flight of steps. Soon after reaching the bottom you come to a T-junction – here turn left along a wooded track that heads downhill, curving to the right and passing a series of pools on the left, to a road.

Turn right uphill and, opposite the entrance to the Hillscourt Conference Centre **G**, turn left to follow a most attractive wooded path to a lane. The Lickey Hills Visitor Centre is a few yards to the left. ●

Lickey Hills – Birmingham's traditional weekend and Bank Holiday playground

Clent Hills

Start	Clent Hills – Nimmings Lane Visitor Centre
Distance	5½ miles (8.9km)
Approximate time	3 hours
Parking	Nimmings Lane Visitor Centre
Refreshments	Pubs and cafés at Clent, light refreshments at visitor centre
Ordnance Survey maps	Landranger 139 (Birmingham), Pathfinders 933, SO 88/98 (Stourbridge and Kinver) and 953, SO 87/97 (Kidderminster & Bromsgrove)

Two splendid ridge sections that give extensive views are the chief highlights of this walk on the 'bald and breezy heights' of the Clent Hills, a traditional Bank Holiday and Sunday afternoon destination for the people of Birmingham and the Black Country. The walk ascends the two main hills, Adam's Hill and Walton Hill, but the gradients are modest and the paths throughout are generally clear and well defined.

At the entrance to the car park, turn right along the road for a few yards and then right again through a wooden barrier. Follow a steep uphill path through fine old beech trees, keeping by a wire fence on the left; after a short sharp climb the path levels out and continues to a barrier on the edge of the woodland. Go through this and turn right along a broad scenic ridge path to reach the 997ft (304m) summit of Adam's Hill, crowned by a triangulation pillar, toposcope and the Four Stones Ⓐ. Although they may look authentic, the Four Stones are not a prehistoric circle but a folly, erected by an 18th-century owner of nearby Hagley Hall. The view from here is magnificent.

Continue along the ridge path, which now heads gently downhill, curving gradually to the left. As you descend, Clent village can be seen below on the right and, at a path junction, turn right and head down towards it. Turn left along the road through the village and shortly

turn half-left along Mount Lane Ⓑ. At a road junction, bear left for just over ¼ mile (400m) to Clent church, mostly rebuilt in the 19th century but retaining its 15th-century tower.

At the crossroads by the church, keep ahead along the lane signposted to Walton Pool and after ¼ mile (400m) turn left through a wooden kissing-gate Ⓒ. Head diagonally across a field to go through a metal kissing-gate at the far end, cross a lane, walk along the drive opposite and, to the right of a pair of metal gates (where the drive starts to curve left to a house), climb a stile. Continue along the left-hand edge of a field, climb one stile and a second a few yards ahead, cross a lane and climb the stile opposite to continue straight across a field. Go through a metal gate and a few yards ahead the path bears left to join another path at a T-junction. Turn right at the T-junction and continue across the field to a stile Ⓓ. However, the Right of Way may be blocked by crops,

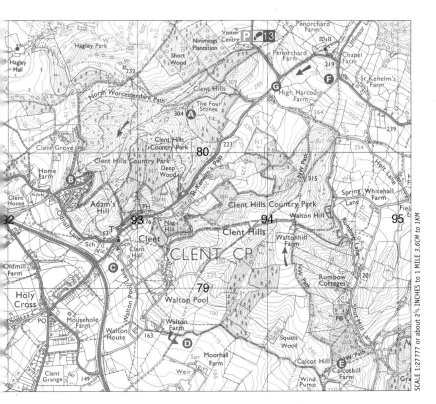

0	200	400	600	800 METRES	1
					KILOMETRES
					MILES
0	200	400	600 YARDS	½	

although there is an obvious, if unofficial, path that continues straight ahead, between the crops to the stile. Climb it and turn left along a track, following it as it curves to the right to keep alongside the right-hand edge of a conifer plantation.

This pleasant track climbs gently over Calcot Hill to reach a metal gate. Go through this and another about 50 yds (46m) ahead and continue to Calcothill Farm. Just in front of the house, turn left over a stile, walk along the right-hand edge of a field to a finger-post and turn right in the direction indicated, keeping by a wire fence on the right, to a stile **E**. Climb it and turn left along the field edge to climb another stile; here joining the North Worcestershire Path.

Now continue along a well-defined path which stays above the top edge of sloping fields. Climb two stiles and, after the second, pass to the right of a farm.

Climb a third stile, turn left along a track to a North Worcestershire Path marker post and turn right across the open expanses of Walton Hill to the triangulation pillar on the 1035ft (315m) summit, another fine vantage-point.

Continue along the ridge path to the end of the ridge, where a North Worcestershire Path marker-post directs you to the right. Descend steeply down steps, across a track, and down more steps to reach a lane. Cross to a footpath sign opposite and continue across a large field, making for a stile in the bottom left-hand corner. Climb this, bear left along a lane **F** and turn left at the first junction to pass Saint Kenelm's Church.

It dates mainly from the 12th-century and was built on the site of the legendary martyrdom of Saint Kenelm, a 9th-century boy king of Mercia who was allegedly killed on the orders of his sister.

Continue past the church and take the first turning on the right **G** to return to the start. ●

Witley Court and Abberley Hill

Start	Great Witley – car park at junction of A443 and B4197
Distance	6½ miles (10.5km). Shorter version 5 miles (8km)
Approximate time	3½ hours (2½ hours for shorter version)
Parking	Great Witley
Refreshments	Pub at Great Witley, pub at Abberley
Ordnance Survey maps	Landranger 138 (Kidderminster & Wyre Forest) and Pathfinder 973, SO 66/76 (Great Witley)

There is considerable historic and scenic appeal on this walk amidst the well-wooded Abberley Hills, which rise to almost 1000ft (305m) above the fields and orchards that lie between the Severn and Teme valleys. Historic interest is provided by the extensive remains of Witley Court, the flamboyant 18th-century church next to it and, in complete contrast, the ruins of the simple Norman church at Abberley. The main scenic attraction is the splendid ridgetop walk along Abberley Hill, which is reached by a fairly steep climb from the starting point at Great Witley. The shorter version of the walk omits an initial detour to visit Witley Court.

If following the shorter version, start with your back to the road and climb a stile on the right-hand side of the car park. Walk along a paved path in front of a building and follow it round to the left to another stile. Climb that and walk diagonally across a field to come out on to a road, turning left to join the longer route just before **B** *below.*

The full walk includes a detour of about 1½ miles (2.4km) to visit Witley Court and church, which is eminently worthwhile. From the car park turn left along the road, take the first turning on the right (signposted 'Witley Court and Church') and then follow a rough broad track for ¾ mile (1.25km) to reach the entrance to Witley Court **A**.

Originally built in the 17th century, Witley Court was rebuilt on a palatial scale by the 1st Earl of Dudley in 1860, but was gutted by fire in 1937. Since then it has stood, a rather melancholic but impressive empty shell, and the remains of its state rooms, orangery, terraces and the gardens still convey something of the former grandeur of this huge palace. The church that adjoins it looks as if it has been transplanted from Italy or Austria. It was built by the 1st Lord Foley in 1735 in the Rococo style; unusual and very un-English but undeniably beautiful with a most ornate and colourful interior.

Retrace your steps back to the road, keep straight ahead on the road, signposted to Stourport, and follow it to a

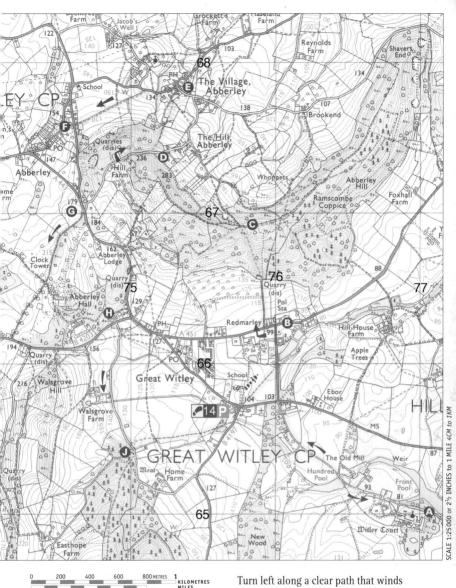

T-junction **B**. Turn left and, at a public bridleway sign to Shavers End, turn right on to a tarmac track. The track soon becomes a sunken path, initially between trees and embankments on both sides, and later continues uphill between orchards. Pass through a gate to a footpath sign just ahead and, ignoring a bridleway turning to the right, keep straight ahead, climbing steeply through woodland to a T-junction of paths **C**.

Turn left along a clear path that winds between trees, take the left-hand upper path at a fork and continue along the wooded ridge, heading uphill to a Worcestershire Way post. Here follow the direction of the yellow waymark slightly to the right to continue along this fine ridge walk, with spectacular views through the trees on both sides, still winding uphill all the time to reach the triangulation pillar at the top of Abberley Hill, 928ft (283m) high. Follow Worcestershire Way signs past the triangulation pillar, now heading

The ruined elegance of Witley Court

downhill, to climb a stile on to a lane.

Turn right and, at a Worcestershire Way sign **D**, turn left to head steeply downhill once more, making directly for Abberley village in front. Climb one stile, turn left along the edge of a field, climb another and continue, crossing a concrete path to a third stile. Climb that, head downhill across a field to climb a stile in the bottom corner and keep ahead a few yards to a track, turning right into the village. In front of you are the remains of a small 12th-century church and to the left you can see the tower and spire of its 19th-century successor, built because by the Victorian era the Norman church was considered to be beyond repair, following centuries of neglect. After the construction of the new church , the earlier building continued to deteriorate until restoration began in 1963. Two doorways and the foundations of the west end belong to the original 12th-century building; the restored chapel is a 14th-century extension.

Turn left along the road to a T-junction **E** and then left again. At a footpath sign to Abberley Common, turn left through a metal kissing-gate and head gently uphill, by a hedge and wire fence on the left, continuing past a now redundant kissing-gate to keep along the right-hand edge of a field. From here there are wide open views, especially to the right looking across to the line of the Clee Hills. On reaching a road **F** turn left and continue for just over $\frac{1}{4}$ mile (400m) to a junction, keep ahead for a few yards and, opposite a lane leading off to the left, turn right on to a track, at a Worcestershire Way sign and public bridleway sign to Stanford Road **G**.

The track heads uphill, passing to the right of an ornate Victorian clock-tower, built in 1883 by the owner of Abberley Hall, which is now a school. At a junction of tracks keep ahead, walking to the right of school buildings, and continue along a broad track lined with trees to pass through the lodge gates of Abberley Hall to a road. Turn left along the road for almost $\frac{1}{2}$ mile (800m) and, just before reaching a junction, turn right along a narrow lane **H**. After about $\frac{1}{2}$ mile (800m) before the road starts to bear to the right, turn left over a stile **J**.

Continue along the field edge to a stile. On the left is a fine view of Abberley Hill. Climb this stile and then a second to walk across the next field towards a pool. Go through a metal gate and keep by the edge of the pool to join a track that leads to a road. Turn left for the short distance back to the start.

Kenilworth and Honiley

Start	Kenilworth
Distance	6½ miles (10.5km)
Approximate time	3½ hours
Parking	Kenilworth – either on Castle Green or by castle entrance
Refreshments	Restaurants, pubs and cafés at Kenilworth
Ordnance Survey maps	Landrangers 139 (Birmingham) and 140 (Leicester, Coventry & Rugby), Pathfinder 955, SP 27/37 (Coventry (South) & Kenilworth)

The extensive and imposing ruins of Kenilworth Castle, in sight for much of the route, are the chief attraction of this easy walk; a less grand but nevertheless interesting building is the early 18th-century church at Honiley, roughly two-thirds of the way round. In between these two focal points the walk crosses a pleasant, fairly flat and open landscape, mostly by well-defined field paths.

The castle dominates old Kenilworth; the modern town centre lies to the east across the open expanse of Abbey Fields. One of the strongest and most impressive medieval fortresses in the country, Kenilworth Castle has had a colourful history, with a succession of royal and baronial owners, and its buildings span over four centuries. At one time it was surrounded by lakes, formed by damming a nearby stream to create additional water defences. The castle was founded by Geoffrey de Clinton in the early 12th century and later in that century the powerful Norman keep was built. After passing into royal ownership it was enlarged and strengthened by both Henry II and John. Henry III gave it to his sister, the wife of Simon de Montfort, a powerful future enemy, and consequently had to besiege it for six months in 1266 in order to recover it from Simon de Montfort's son. Later it came into the possession of the earls and dukes of Lancaster, and John

of Gaunt built the 14th-century Banqueting Hall, one of the finest of its kind. The accession of the Duke of Lancaster as Henry IV in 1399 caused the castle to revert to the Crown again until Elizabeth I presented it to her favourite, Robert Dudley, Earl of Leicester, in 1563. Dudley began the conversion of the castle into a more comfortable and palatial residence, building the 16th-century gatehouse, and in 1575 entertained the Queen here on a lavish scale and at huge cost for nineteen days, with feasting, music and firework displays. After the Civil War between Crown and Parliament, the castle was slighted and subsequently fell into ruin.

Not far away across Abbey Fields are the mainly 15th-century church and sparse remains of Kenilworth Abbey, which are both (like the castle) built of warm-looking red sandstone.

If you are starting at Castle Green, a pleasant spot with a row of attractive old cottages, face the castle and turn left to go through a kissing-gate at a Centenary Way sign and follow a path alongside the castle walls. Go up some steps to the present entrance to the castle and turn left along a causeway towards the car park – this is the alternative starting point.

At a Centenary Way sign in front of the car park, turn right (turn left if starting from here) along a track for a few yards and bear right to climb a stile, at a footpath sign to Beausale **A**. For the next part of the walk detailed route directions are unnecessary, as you follow clear and well-waymarked field paths, sometimes along the edge and sometimes across the middle of a succession of fields, over a series of well-maintained stiles, with open views all around over a typical Warwickshire landscape of fields and hedges, woods and low hills. Watch for a meeting of paths, where you follow the direction of a waymark half-left (not fully to the left), to pass through a hedge gap and continue along the left-hand edge of a field to another hedge gap. Here turn sharp right along the left-hand edge of a field, by a hedge on the left, shortly turning left over a stile. Continue in a straight line across the middle of three more fields, joining a track at the end of the third field and, passing to the left of a farm, follow the track to a lane **B**.

Turn right and follow the lane around a left-hand bend into Beausale. At a crossroads, turn right along the road signposted to Honiley, taking the first turning on the right **C** after just over $1/4$ mile (400m). On entering Honiley, and at the point where the road bends to the left, a short detour to the right brings you

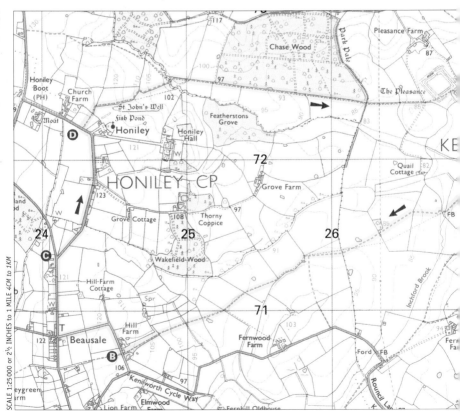

to the church, a rare and interesting example of an 18th-century village church, built in 1723 by John Sanders of the now-demolished Honiley House. There is a story that the church was designed by Sir Christopher Wren, who owned nearby Wroxall Abbey, on a tablecloth while dining with John Sanders, but it is more likely that it was designed by Francis Smith, a local Warwick architect.

The imposing ruins of Kenilworth Castle

The route continues along the road for another 50 yds (46m) before turning right over a stile at a public footpath sign **D**. Head across the middle of a field, go through a hedge gap and continue along the right-hand edge of the next field. Look out for a gap and waymark in the hedge on the right, go through the gap and continue along the right-hand edge of a field by a hedge on the right, heading downhill. In front is Chase Wood and from here there is also the first distant glimpse of Kenilworth Castle on this return leg.

Follow the curving field edge to cross a footbridge over a brook and keep ahead, bearing right along the left-hand edge of a field. Continue along the left-hand edge of several fields to a stile, climb over and keep ahead along the left-hand edge of the next field to another stile. Climb it and now continue along the right-hand edge of a field to climb a stile and bear left across the next field, making your way through the earthworks of The Pleasance, site of a 15th-century royal pleasure-palace, to a stile and public footpath sign on the far side.

Climb the stile and walk along a partly hedge- and tree-lined path which, after passing to the left of a farm, widens into a track. Continue along this track, from which there are superb views of the castle, heading up to the starting point at Castle Green and on the way passing a most attractive cottage. ●

Great Malvern and the Worcestershire Beacon

Start	Great Malvern
Distance	5½ miles (8.9km)
Approximate time	3 hours
Parking	Great Malvern
Refreshments	Pubs and cafés at Great Malvern, café at St Ann's Well
Ordnance Survey maps	Landranger 150 (Worcester & The Malverns) and Explorer 14 (Malvern Hills)

This walk climbs from Great Malvern to the highest point, the Worcestershire Beacon, and continues along the ridge, before descending and returning along paths that contour around the wooded lower slopes of the hills. This is Elgar country; the great composer was born and lived most of his life within sight of the Malverns. The hills are honeycombed with paths and it can be difficult to keep to a precise route because of this. But provided you avoid the hills in misty weather, the various settlements that encircle them are in sight for most of the time and there are also a number of stone direction indicators, erected by the Malvern Hills Conservators, to show the way down.

Rising abruptly from the flat lands of the Vale of Severn in the east and the rolling hills of Herefordshire in the west, the Malvern Hills resemble a mountain range, despite reaching only 1395ft (425m). The Regency and Victorian hotels and villas that cover their slopes reflect the heyday of Great Malvern as a popular spa and health resort. Much older is the grand priory church in the town centre, founded in 1085. The nave is Norman, and the rest of the church is a fine example of the Perpendicular style of the 15th century.

Start at the meeting of roads in the centre of Great Malvern, just to the north of the priory, and walk along Belle Vue Terrace in the Worcester direction, turning left along St Ann's Road. This narrow road heads steeply uphill and later becomes a tarmac track which continues up through the steep-sided, tree-lined Happy Valley. Where the tarmac track swings sharply to the left at a junction of several tracks **Ⓐ**, turn sharp right, at a stone indicator to Ivy Scar Rock, and a few yards ahead bear right along a broad track which winds round the lower slopes of the wooded hills.

Keep on the main track all the while, climbing gently to pass to the right of Ivy Scar Rock. A few yards beyond the wooden bench below the rock, bear slightly left on to a narrower uphill path between gorse, scrub and bracken, following it around a series of zigzag bends to reach a T-junction. Here turn right along a grand, broad, flat track – Lady Howard De Walden Drive. At a fork the drive continues along the left-hand uphill track; follow as it curves first to the left around North Hill, and later to both right and left around Table Hill.

At a fork just before a left-hand bend, take the uphill track to the left which heads over Table Hill – the houses of West Malvern are below on the right – to reach a junction of tracks. Keep ahead until you join a broad, clear, stony track by a sharp bend and turn right to follow it towards the summit of the Worcestershire Beacon. At a crossroads keep ahead and, at a circular stone indicator where several alternative routes to the Beacon are shown, it is probably easiest to keep along the main track. This curves upwards and finally turns sharp right to reach the triangulation pillar, sheltered picnic area and circular toposcope on the 1395ft (425m) summit. This is the highest point on the Malverns and an inevitably superb all-round viewpoint **B**.

From the summit continue along the ridge path, with grand views on both sides and a spectacular view of the Malverns in front. Descend to join a tarmac track and follow it gently downhill to reach another circular stone indicator **C**. Turn sharp left in the direction of 'Quarry Walk and St Ann's Well via Earnslaw' along a wooded track. At a fork take the left-hand, broader grassy track that heads gently uphill again to pass above a huge, deep quarry on the right, which is landscaped with a pool at the bottom. Soon the track zigzags steeply downhill to a spot near the bottom of the quarry **D**. Do not take the last sharp turn to the right, which leads to the quarry, but keep ahead along a much narrower path – take care here as the ground slopes steeply away from the path in places – which winds and undulates through woodland along the side of the hill to a path junction.

Here bear slightly right, ignoring two descending paths on the immediate right, to continue along a steadily ascending

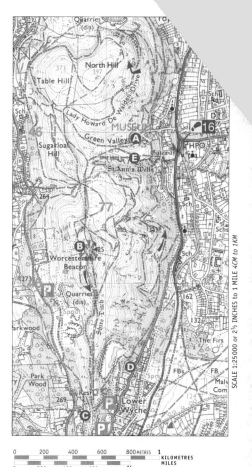

SCALE 1:25000 or 2½ INCHES to 1 MILE 4CM to 1KM

path, taking the right-hand path at a fork by a metal seat. This wooded path heads gently downhill, curving right, below the face of the hill, to join a track. Continue along the track, which winds through more woodland, to St Ann's Well. In the 19th century, buildings were erected over the well for the use of the increasing number of visitors coming to take the waters; nowadays they serve as a café.

At the well **E**, turn right to follow the broad tarmac track which winds downhill to a lane. Turn right, at a footpath sign, down a drive towards a large house, and go down some steps to the left of the gatewayof the house, turning left and continuing down a flight of steps to reach the road in front of the Abbey Hotel and priory. Turn left back to the start.

Shugborough Park, Sherbrook Valley and Brocton Coppice

Start	Milford Common
Distance	7 miles (11.3km)
Approximate time	3½ hours
Parking	Milford Common
Refreshments	Pub and café at Milford Common, pub and café at Great Haywood
Ordnance Survey maps	Landrangers 127 (Stafford & Telford) and 128 (Derby & Burton upon Trent), Explorer 6 (Cannock Chase)

A remarkable variety of scenery and a wide range of historic attractions are featured in this modest but highly attractive walk on the north-western fringes of Cannock Chase. The former embraces landscaped parkland, canal and riverside meadows, conifer forest, open heathland and the finest remaining area of traditional oakwood in the chase. The latter includes an 18th-century mansion, 17th-century pack-horse bridge and part of a disused railway built in World War I.

Cannock, or Cank, Forest originally covered a large area between Stafford in the west and Tamworth in the east, and from the Trent valley in the north to Wolverhampton and Walsall in the south. It was a royal forest, but in 1290 Edward I granted part of it to the bishops of Lichfield as their private chase. In the 16th century, ownership passed to the Paget family (later the marquises of Anglesey), who pioneered the development of the local iron industry. Demands for charcoal for iron smelting led to the felling of many of the woodlands, and much of the chase became bare heathland until the 1920s, when the Forestry Commission began large-scale conifer plantations, mostly of pine. Cannock Chase is now chiefly heath and conifer forest, but some

older broadleaved woodland remains, mostly in the area of this walk.

Start by heading across Milford Common to the main road and turn right, passing the entrance to Shugborough Hall on the left. Shortly, turn left by a wall on the left, which soon becomes a wire fence, following a path that climbs between bracken and a superb array of silver birches. Bear right at the top of the hill when the path divides, away from the railings guarding the covered reservoir. Then keep in a straight line ahead, descending to rejoin the road. Turn left along it for about ¼ mile (400m) and, at a public bridleway sign to Great Haywood, turn left through a gate **A**, pass through another about 50 yds (46m) further on and continue straight ahead along a

0	200	400	600	800 METRES	**1**
					KILOMETRES
					MILES
0	200	400	600 YARDS	½	

SCALE 1:27 777 or about 2¼ INCHES to 1 MILE 3.6CM to 1KM

tarmac drive across Shugborough Park, which is now owned by the National Trust and administered by Staffordshire County Council, although part of the house is still occupied by the Earl of Lichfield.

To the left there is a view of the Anson Arch, built to commemorate Admiral George Anson's circumnavigation of the world in the 1740s. It was largely from the profits of this voyage that George's brother, Thomas Anson, an ancestor of the present Earl of Lichfield, was able to landscape the park and enlarge and complete the house.

Cross a railway line and where the drive divides take the left-hand fork, passing to the right of Park Farm, which is now a farm museum. Soon the elegant Shugborough Hall can be seen to the left;

where the main drive bears left towards it, go through a gate and continue straight ahead along a narrower track to reach the 17th-century Essex Bridge over the River Trent **B**. This fourteen-arched bridge was built by an earl of Essex to allow easier access to the chase for his hunting parties. Cross it, and here the route turns right, along the towpath of the Trent and Mersey Canal, but a brief detour ahead crossing the canal bridge and under a railway bridge leads into the village of Great Haywood.

The towpath makes very pleasant walking, initially squeezing between the river on the right and the canal on the left, with fine views across meadows looking towards Shugborough Hall. After passing under a road bridge, leave the canal by climbing some steps on the right and turning left along the road **C**, following it under the railway and over the Trent to meet the main road again. Cross over and take the track ahead, which leads uphill into woodland to the pleasant parking and picnic area of Seven Springs. Here turn right, passing a forestry barrier and, where the track forks a few yards ahead, take the right-hand broader track. Bear right at the next fork and continue along an undulating track through a mixed area of heathland, broadleaved woodland and conifer plantations. Eventually the track descends gently into the Sherbrook valley

Essex Bridge over the River Trent

at the 'Stepping Stones' This is an idyllic spot which has widely scattered trees interspersed with grassy glades which are surrounded by wooded slopes.

Cross the brook by the stepping-stones and turn left on to the Staffordshire Way **D** to walk through the delightful Sherbrook valley; the woodland later gives way to more open country of bracken- and heather-covered slopes dotted with random groups of trees. It is easy to see why this is considered to be the most beautiful valley in the chase. Ignore the first broad track on the right and about 250 yds (228m) further on – by a picnic area and Staffordshire Way sign – turn sharp right along a track **E** which soon curves to the left and heads uphill between banks of heather and bracken.

At the top the track curves to the right to continue to a forestry barrier and on to a broad track beyond. Turn right, passing through a car park, and pass another forestry barrier, ignoring the left-hand turn just past it, and continue to where the track forks **F**. At this point turn left along another track which heads downhill between the ancient oaks of Brocton Coppice, the most extensive area of oak forest remaining in Cannock Chase.

Eventually turn left to join a broad track and turn right along it as it curves above Mere Pool on the left. This track was once part of the 'Tackeroo Railway', built in World War I in order to carry supplies to the two huge military camps established at the time on the chase. At a crossroads of several tracks and paths keep straight ahead, following directions to Milford, through a deep cutting. The track continues to a road, but before reaching it – soon after passing a forestry barrier – bear right **G** on to a track which heads steadily uphill, passing to the left of a small pool. On arriving at the top you can enjoy a fine view ahead over the Trent valley before you descend gently back to Milford Common. ●

Bridgnorth and the River Severn

Start	Bridgnorth
Distance	8½ miles (13.7km)
Approximate time	4½ hours
Parking	Bridgnorth
Refreshments	Pubs and cafés at Bridgnorth
Ordnance Survey maps	Landranger 138 (Kidderminster & Wyre Forest) and Pathfinder 911, SO 69/79 (Bridgnorth & Much Wenlock)

This walk falls into two distinct parts. Starting from Bridgnorth, the route initially takes you through woodland, across fields and along lanes, passing through the village of Astley Abbots, to reach the banks of the River Severn. The second part is an attractive 3¼ mile (5.2km) riverside walk along one of the most scenic and tranquil stretches of the Severn, with fine views of the hilltop town of Bridgnorth towards the end.

Bridgnorth is divided into Low Town and High Town, linked by several sets of steps and, for the less energetic, a cliff railway. It is an attractive and interesting town with a number of 16th- and 17th-century black-and-white half-timbered buildings, some fine churches (including one designed by Telford), a 17th-century town hall, a medieval gateway and a Norman castle whose keep tilts at a greater angle than the Leaning Tower of Pisa. Several vantage-points in High Town give spectacular views over the Severn valley.

Start at the Town Hall and walk northwards, passing under the medieval gateway and along North Gate. About 50 yds (46m) past the gateway the road heads downhill but you keep ahead along a tarmac path above the road, bearing left to rejoin the road opposite a car park. Continue along the road for just over ¼ mile (400m), keeping ahead along

Queensway Road at a junction and taking the first turning on the left (Duchess Drive) **Ⓐ**.

Follow the road as it bends to the right through a modern housing area, climbing gently to a T-junction. Turn left, turn first right into Hook Farm Road and take the first turning on the right. After a few yards the road ends and you continue along the broad track ahead, at a public footpath sign. From the track there are pleasant views to the right and after descending slightly to cross a brook, turn left over a stile. Walk along the left-hand edge of a field, keeping alongside the brook, later heading across to a stile. Climb over the stile and continue along an attractive wooded path, eventually climbing over another stile on to a narrow lane **Ⓑ**.

Turn right along this lane for ½ mile (800m), passing to the right of Tasley

The peaceful Severn near Bridgnorth

church, and where the lane bends to the left, turn right along the track to Kingsley Farm ●. Just before reaching the farm buildings, turn right through a metal gate at a public footpath sign and walk along the right-hand edge of a field, by a hedge on the right. Go through another metal gate and continue along the right-hand edge of the next field, by a wire fence and woodland on the right, heading downhill into the valley of Cantern Brook. Cross a footbridge over the brook and continue uphill across the next field – there is no obvious path – later joining and keeping by a wire fence and trees on the right.

In the top corner of the field turn right through a waymarked metal gate and take the enclosed track ahead, passing to the left of a house. Pass through a metal gate and continue between houses to a road ●. Cross over the road and take the lane opposite, signposted to Astley Abbots and Colemore Green, following it for just over ¹⁄₂ mile (800m) into the sleepy village of Astley Abbots, which possesses some attractive black-and-white houses and a partly Norman church. Continue through the village and, shortly after passing a lane on the left, turn right over a half-hidden, waymarked stile by a metal gate ●. Walk along the right-hand edge of a field, by a fence on the right, climb two

stiles – crossing the intervening plank over a ditch – and continue along the right-hand edge of a field, turning right over a stile in the field corner. Keep ahead for a few yards to climb another stile and turn left along the left-hand edge of a field, by a wire fence on the left. Bear left on joining a grassy track, follow it between fields and past pools to a farm and, in front of a house, turn right between farm buildings, then left, go through a metal gate and follow the farm drive to a lane.

Turn right and after 300 yds (274m) turn left over a stile ● and walk along the left-hand edge of a field. Go through a gate to enter the woodland of Chestnut Coppice and follow a track through

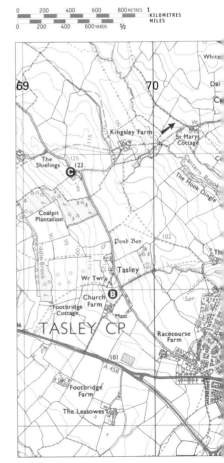

conifers, heading downhill and keeping in a straight line along the main track all the while. Bear right to cross the track of a disused railway, go through a gate and keep ahead for a few yards across the grass to reach the River Severn **G**.

Turn right to follow the placid river for 3¼ miles (5.2km) back to Bridgnorth – a lovely stretch of riverside walking over a series of stiles and with steep wooded slopes on the opposite bank all the way. Initially there are wooded slopes on the right of the river too, but later you continue across meadows, then by the edge of a golf course and finally alongside a playing-field. Towards the end of this stretch come good views of the churches and houses of Bridgnorth, high above the river. So peaceful is the river nowadays that it is difficult to believe that in the 18th century, before the advent of canals and later railways, there was a great deal of both passenger and commercial traffic on the Severn from Shrewsbury and Coalbrookdale in the north down to Bewdley, Worcester, Gloucester and the Bristol Channel.

After leaving the playing-field, continue along a track that leads to a road and follow the road to the old bridge over the Severn **H**. Here turn right towards the cliff railway and either take the railway or climb steps that wind upwards to High Town, turning left at the top to reach the High Street a few yards to the left of the Town Hall.

SCALE 1:27777 or about 2¼ INCHES to 1 MILE 3.6CM to 1KM

Bidford-on-Avon, Cleeve Prior and Middle Littleton

Bidford-on-Avon, Cleeve Prior and Middle Littleton

Start	Bidford-on-Avon
Distance	8 miles (12.9km)
Approximate time	4 hours
Parking	Bidford-on-Avon
Refreshments	Pubs and cafés at Bidford-on-Avon, pub at Cleeve Prior, pub at North Littleton
Ordnance Survey maps	Landranger 150 (Worcester & The Malverns), Pathfinders 997, SP 05/15 (Stratford-upon-Avon (West) & Alcester) and 1020, SP 04/14 (Vale of Evesham)

The route first crosses fields and meadows, passing through Marlcliff and Cleeve Prior, to the villages of North and Middle Littleton. From here a gentle climb on to a ridge is followed by a fine ridgetop walk of almost 3 miles (4.8km) above the winding River Avon back to Marlcliff. Despite its modest height of around 220ft (67m), the ridge reveals outstanding views across the orchard and market-gardening country of the Vale of Evesham to Bredon Hill, the Cotswolds and the Malverns. A final pleasant stroll is across riverside meadows back to Bidford-on-Avon.

The view of Bidford-on-Avon from the river is most attractive. Houses are massed above the riverbank, with the 15th-century stone bridge over the River Avon in the foreground and the tower of the restored medieval church behind.

Start on the south side of the old bridge over the Avon by entering the riverside recreation ground. Bear left along its left-hand edge, by a hedge on the left, go through a kissing-gate and follow a clear path across the middle of a field to climb a stile. Continue along the left-hand edge of the next field, by a hedge on the left, turn left over a stile and ditch and walk along the right-hand edge of a field, by trees on the right. Climb another stile, keep along the right-hand edge of the next field, by a

fence on the right, go through a gap and continue between fences on both sides, over another stile and on into the village of Marlcliff, a harmonious mixture of modern houses and old black-and-white thatched cottages.

Keep ahead to join a lane and at a junction bear right **Ⓐ**, passing to the right of the thatched cottage in front. Go through a gate and follow a short but steep climb up Marlcliff Hill. At the top keep ahead across grass to climb one stile and continue across a field to climb another. Bear slightly left across the next field, climb a stile and follow a path across the next one, continuing by the left-hand edge of an orchard to pass through a hedge gap. Bear left across a

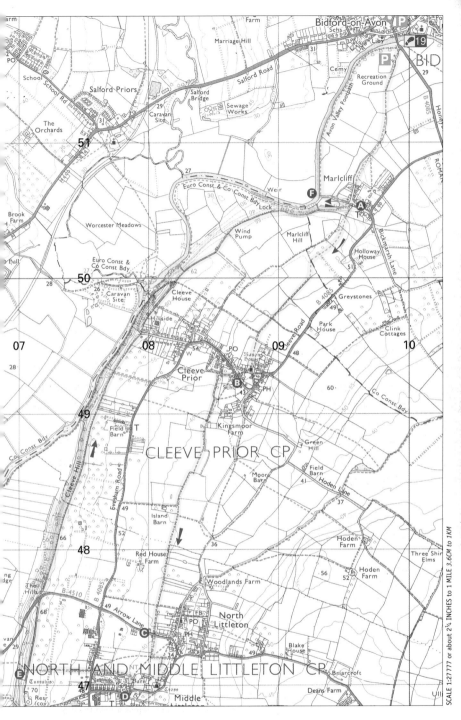

to pass through a gap in a fence. Continue, still by a hedge on the right, cross a footbridge over a brook and bear slightly left across the next field, heading directly towards Cleeve Prior church.

field to a stile in the far corner, climb this and keep ahead, by a hedge on the right,

Climb one stile, keep ahead and climb another to enter the churchyard. Bear right to pass in front of the church, going through a metal kissing-gate and on to the road by the village green

Church and old bridge over the Avon at Bidford

Cleeve Prior is pleasant and sleepy, and rather like a Cotswold village, with many stone houses and cottages and an impressive 13th- to 14th-century church. Cross the road and at a public footpath sign to North Littleton continue along the track opposite, which soon bends to the left at a public footpath sign to Middle Littleton. Keep along the track; at first it is hedge-lined, then it continues along the left-hand edge of a field and passes through a hedge gap. It bears right by a line of trees on the left, turns left over a footbridge and continues along the right-hand edge of fields.

Keep in a straight line – later switching to walk along the left-hand edge of fields – to emerge eventually on to a lane on the edge of North Littleton **C**. Turn left for the pub; otherwise cross the lane and take the path ahead, between fields, turning right over a stile. Now turn left and immediately left again over another stile, keep along the edge of a field, by a hedge on the left and, where you see a stile on the left, turn right and head across the field, making directly towards Middle Littleton church. The view ahead is dominated by a large tithe barn, 136ft (41m) long, which belonged to the monks of Evesham Abbey and is now a National Trust property. Climb a stile and continue through the churchyard, passing to the left of the church and going through a metal kissing-gate on to a lane.

Turn right and where the lane bends to the left turn right again **D**, at a public footpath sign to Cleeve Prior and a sign to the tithe barn, along a tarmac track. Climb

the stile in front, turn left along the left-hand edge of a field, keeping by garden fences, climb another stile and continue, then climb a third stile on to a road. Cross over, climb the stile opposite and keep along the right-hand edge of a field, by a fence on the right. Where that fence ends, continue straight ahead, climbing gently on to a ridge **E**. From this modest ridge, of only 220ft (67m), you can enjoy a magnificent view ahead across the Vale of Evesham, with the Avon winding beneath you, the Malverns on the horizon and Bredon Hill and the Cotswold escarpment to the left.

Turn right and now follow a superb ridgetop walk of almost 3 miles (4.8km) to Marlcliff. The track, which can be muddy at times, is well waymarked; it crosses one road and later a narrow lane. It is hedge- and tree-lined in places but the many gaps reveal superb views on both sides, outstanding ones to the left over the Avon valley. Eventually you descend Marlcliff Hill, bearing left through a gate into the village and momentarily rejoining the outward route **A**.

At a public bridleway sign turn left along a track to the river and, just before reaching it, turn right over a footbridge to climb a waymarked stile **F**. Keep along the riverbank back to Bidford – a flat, easy stroll – climbing a series of stiles and finally following the edge of the recreation ground to return to the starting point by the bridge. ●

Bewdley and Wyre Forest

Start	Bewdley
Distance	8 miles (12.9km)
Approximate time	4 hours
Parking	Bewdley
Refreshments	Pubs and cafés at Bewdley
Ordnance Survey maps	Landranger 138 (Kidderminster & Wyre Forest) and Pathfinder 952, SO 67/77 (Wyre Forest & Cleobury Mortimer)

The first ¾ mile (1.25km) of this walk is along the banks of the River Severn, most of the remainder is through the lovely woodlands of Wyre Forest, one of the forests of the Midlands that has managed to survive centuries of felling, chiefly to serve the needs of the local iron industries of the Black Country. From the higher points there are grand views over the Severn valley and neighbouring hills. Although quite lengthy, this is an easy walk with just a few modest climbs, though muddy sections are likely to be encountered on some of the woodland tracks.

Bewdley was described by the 16th-century antiquarian Leland as a 'most delightful town, whom Wyre's tall oaks with lofty leafage crown'. It is very much a Georgian town, with a number of 17th- and 18th-century houses, a mostly 18th-century church and an elegant bridge over the River Severn built by Telford (1795–8). The fine Georgian quaysides reflect the town's importance as an inland port before the river trade dwindled in the face of competition from the canals, which came to nearby Stourport, as well as from the railways.

Start on the north side of the bridge by going down some steps and walking along the former quay of Severn Side North. At a public footpath sign keep ahead along a pleasant, broad and well-constructed riverside path, part of the Worcestershire Way. Climb a stile, continue by the river and just in front of the supports of a former railway bridge, climb another stile, cross a footbridge over Dowles Brook Ⓐ and turn left to follow a track beside the brook up to a road.

Turn right for about 100 yds (91m) and, at a footpath sign, turn left along a path that heads through woodland, keeping below the embankment of a disused railway on the left and by a wire fence on the right. The rest of the walk is mostly through Wyre Forest, a medieval royal hunting-ground that formerly extended over a large area of Shropshire and Worcestershire between Bridgnorth and Worcester, and gave its name to Worcestershire (Wyre-castra). Although much smaller than before and nowadays partly comprising conifer plantations, the forest covers an extensive area of around 6000 acres (of which 2800 are managed by the Forestry Commission) and there still remain many areas of splendid

SCALE 1:31 250 or 2 INCHES to 1 MILE 3.2CM to 1KM

```
0    200   400   600   800 METRES 1
                                    KILOMETRES
                                    MILES
0    200   400   600 YARDS   ½
```

deciduous woodlands. The next 1½ miles (2.4km) is through the valley of Dowles Brook, regarded by many as the most attractive part of the forest.

The path crosses the brook and continues to a T-junction. Here turn right along a track, take the right-hand track at a fork, recross Dowles Brook and continue through the delightful, narrow, steep-sided and thickly wooded valley with the brook gurgling below on the left.

Pass to the right of Knowles Mill, one of a number of watermills that once occupied the valley, pass beside a metal gate and continue through a more open area beside a sloping meadow on the left. Keep ahead on joining another track, passing to the right of Cooper's Mill Youth Centre, and shortly afterwards – just before the track reaches the brow of a hill – turn left **B** and head down to cross a footbridge over Dowles Brook once more. Turn right and walk alongside the brook for about 50 yds (46m) and then follow the path as it bears left and heads uphill, bearing left all the while (almost to the point of doing a U-turn) before passing through a gate and crossing a disused railway track.

Bear slightly right to go through the right-hand of two gates in front and continue along a clear track through Shelf Held Coppice. The track heads steadily uphill, then levels off and you keep along it in a straight line amidst a most attractive traditional forest landscape. On reaching a field on the right, turn right to follow a path along the right-hand edge of that field, by a wire fence on the left and, after joining a track, keep ahead to plunge once more into thick woodland. The track curves left and meanders through Lord's Yard Coppice. At a fork just before the edge of the woods, take the right-hand path, keeping by a wire fence bordering a field on the left, pass through a gap beside a gate and continue along a broad track to emerge on to a road ❸.

Turn left along it for nearly ¹/₂ mile (800m), soon heading gently downhill and, just after passing a former church (now a private house) on the right, turn right along a lane ❹. At a public footpath sign to the Frank Chapman Centre, bear left on to a track, passing to the left of a bungalow. The track runs alongside the edge of woodland, then curves first left and then right to continue through the trees. A few yards before reaching a field in front, follow the track as it bears right to a metal gate. Do not go through the gate, but turn left in front of it (yellow waymark) along a hedge- and tree-lined track to a lane ❺ – here there is a fine view over the Severn valley.

Turn left along the lane and opposite a stile on the left, turn right through a hedge gap and walk across a large field, keeping in a straight line and heading towards the edge of the woodland on the left. Aim for a gap in the hedge at the far end of the field, go through it and turn left to join the Worcestershire Way. Keep along the right-hand edge of woodland and at a Worcestershire Way sign, turn left along a track through the trees to rejoin the lane.

Turn right and follow the lane around a left-hand bend. After ¹/₄ mile (400m) bear right along a broad track ❻, at a Worcestershire Way footpath sign and, at the point where the track curves left to a house, keep ahead to climb a stile and continue along a grassy path, by a hedge on the left. Climb a second stile, continue along a narrow downhill path to climb a third and ahead there is a superb view of the winding River Severn, with hills beyond and the idyllic Ribbesford church immediately below.

Continue down to the church, curving left to climb a stile and then turning right through the churchyard. Ribbesford church was mostly rebuilt after being struck by lightning in 1877, but retains some Norman features and an unusual timber arcade dating from a 15th-century rebuilding. Keeping to the left of the church, go through a gate and turn left along a broad track ❼. To return to Bewdley, you follow the 'Coffin Route', along which the dead were carried from Bewdley church for burial at Ribbesford. Pass under a road bridge, continue to a lane, cross over and go through a kissing-gate opposite, by a public footpath sign. Now continue along a pleasant, gently descending track across sloping fields lined by trees on the right and, where the track curves left through a gate, keep straight ahead along a path. Soon the houses of Bewdley come into sight.

The path joins and keeps by a fence on the left – on the other side of the fence there is a pool. By a Worcestershire Way Information Board go through a metal kissing-gate, continue to where the path forks (at a Worcestershire Way sign) and take the right-hand narrow path, by a wire fence on the left and hedge on the right, continuing between walls and houses to a road. Turn left into the town centre of Bewdley and, reaching the church, turn right down the main street to return to the bridge. ●

Ludlow, Bromfield and Bringewood Chase

Start	Ludlow
Distance	9 miles (14.5km). Shorter version 7½ miles (12.1km)
Approximate time	4½ hours (3½ hours for shorter version)
Parking	Ludlow
Refreshments	Restaurants, pubs and cafés at Ludlow, pub at Bromfield
Ordnance Survey maps	Landranger 137 (Ludlow & Wenlock Edge) and Pathfinder 951, SO 47/57 (Ludlow)

From Ludlow the first part of the walk keeps above the River Teme through the lovely Oakly Park, continuing through the park for a detour to Bromfield with its old priory gatehouse. Next you head across farmland, via the isolated hamlet of Lady Halton, to ascend the wooded ridge of Bringewood Chase, part of the Forestry Commission's Mortimer Forest. A pleasant walk through woodland leads to Whitcliffe Common – from which there is a magnificent view over Ludlow, backed by the Clee Hills – before returning to the town. The shorter version of the walk omits the detour to Bromfield.

Wide streets lined by dignified houses, many of them Georgian, rise steeply from the banks of the River Teme to the town centre of Ludlow, dominated by church and castle. Ludlow Castle was one of the great border fortresses and, as the residence of the Lords President of the Council of Wales from the 16th century onwards, was virtually the capital of Wales for a time. Its extensive walls and towers occupy a fine defensive site above the river and its buildings span several centuries. Some of the walls of the original 11th-century castle of the De Lacys survive, as does a rare and exquisite circular 12th-century Norman chapel. In the 13th century the castle was considerably enlarged – the superb Great Hall belongs to this period – and further

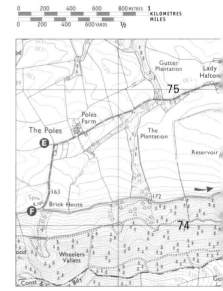

improvements were made in the 16th century in order to turn the medieval castle into a more palatial residence.

The cruciform church, one of the country's largest and most handsome parish churches, with a tall central tower, is approached through a maze of narrow streets and alleys. It is a fine example of a prosperous, mostly 15th-century town church and its unusually wide and spacious interior is of cathedral-like proportions. A.E. Housman is buried in the churchyard.

Start in Castle Square by facing the castle entrance and turning left along a road which follows the line of the castle walls, turning right, bearing left downhill and then right to cross Dinham Bridge. The road then bends to the right and, at a fork, continue along the right-hand lower road. By the Cliffe Hotel climb a waymarked stile **A** and turn half-right to follow a field path gently uphill. Bear left to keep along the right-hand edge of the field, which is bordered by trees – through the trees are splendid views of the meandering River Teme below.

Climb a stile and continue – a fallen treetrunk enables you to get over a wire fence a few yards ahead – along the right-

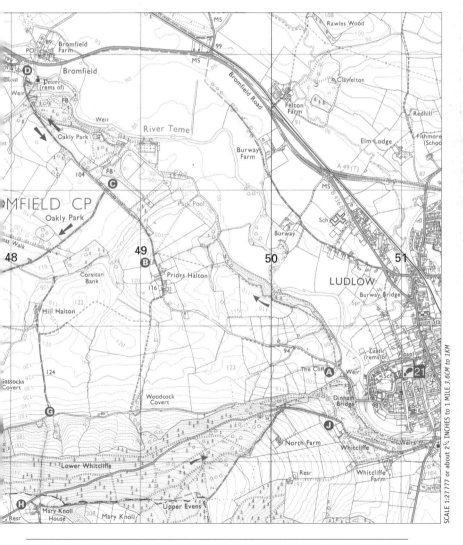

SCALE 1:27777 or about 2¼ INCHES to 1 MILE 3.6CM to 1KM

hand edge of a field, following it as it curves to the left. Here climb a fence on the right and continue along the meandering right-hand edge of the next field, which is bordered by woodland. Climb a stile and keep ahead, following the field edge as it bends to the left. Look out for a footbridge over a brook and a stile below on the right, cross both and turn right along the field edge, following it around to the left and passing a ruined barn. At the end of the field go through a hedge gap on the right and continue in the same direction, now along the left-hand edge of a field, towards the buildings of Priors Halton. Follow the field edge to the right and, in the corner of the field, turn left along a hedge-enclosed track to go through a metal gate on to a tarmac drive **B**.

Turn right, pass beside a metal gate and continue along this lovely tree-lined drive through Oakly Park, once the chase belonging to Ludlow Castle, to a public bridleway sign **C**.

*At this point, those wishing to do the shorter version of the walk should turn left along another tarmac drive, following the main route after **C** below.*

For the full walk, keep straight ahead for another ³⁄₄ mile (1.25km) to cross the River Teme into Bromfield **D**. On the right you pass the 14th-century half-timbered priory gatehouse and beyond that is the church, occupying a promontory between the Rivers Teme and Onny and on the site of a 12th-century Benedictine priory.

Retrace your steps to the public bridleway sign and turn right **C**. Follow the tarmac track as it curves left into the hamlet of Lady Halton, which has a number of attractive black-and-white houses. In the hamlet follow the track to the right – it now becomes a rough farm track – soon passing along the right-hand edge of woodland. Keep ahead, passing to the left of Poles Farm, and shortly

afterwards turn left **E** to continue along a hedge-lined track up to a tarmac track to the left of a house **F**.

Turn left along this track, from which there are fine views to the left across the Teme and Onny valleys towards Wenlock Edge. After just over 1 mile (1.6km) look out for a public bridleway sign **G**, where you turn right through a metal gate and head uphill in a straight line towards conifer woodland. Go through another metal gate to enter the wood, cross a track, continue along an uphill path, cross another track and keep ahead to a road.

Turn right for 50 yds (46m) and go through the first gate on the left **H**. Walk along a path, passing to the left of a house, and climb two stiles in quick succession – both of them to the right of metal gates. Continue gently uphill, by a hedge bank on the right, go through a metal gate to enter the woodlands of Bringewood Chase and follow a path through the trees. Bear slightly left in front of a metal gate and, ignoring all Forestry Commission trails to left and right, keep along the main path, heading gently downhill to reach a broad forestry track. Cross this; there are several tracks in front but keep straight ahead along a sunken track, which later bears left along the edge of woodland to a gate. Go through, continue along a narrow, uneven and likely to be muddy path to join a track and bear right to a road.

Turn right for ¹⁄₄ mile (400m) to a road junction by the parking area of Whitcliffe Common **J**, a popular place for picnics, and a fine vantage point overlooking Ludlow, with the Clee Hills beyond. There are many routes from the common down to the River Teme, but bear left downhill across the grass in the direction of the castle, turn left on reaching a path and follow it through trees. Soon you turn right to head steeply downhill to Dinham Bridge; cross it and retrace your steps uphill to Castle Square. ●

Wenlock Edge

Start	National Trust car park at Wenlock Edge, off B4371 about ¾ mile (1.25km) from centre of Much Wenlock
Distance	8 miles (12.9km)
Approximate time	4 hours
Parking	National Trust car park
Refreshments	None
Ordnance Survey maps	Landranger 138 (Kidderminster & Wyre Forest), Pathfinders 910, SO 49/59 (Church Stretton) and 911, SO 69/79 (Bridgnorth & Much Wenlock)

The long limestone ridge of Wenlock Edge runs for about 15 miles (24km) from Much Wenlock south-westwards towards Craven Arms. From its thickly wooded crest the views, westwards across to Caer Caradoc and the Long Mynd, and northwards to the distinctive profile of the Wrekin, are superb – traditional English landscape at its best. The first part of the route is along the Edge, followed by a descent through woodland and along a lane into the village of Hughley. Then comes a walk along tracks and field paths at its base, and finally a short climb back through woodland to regain the top of the Edge. Nowadays much of Wenlock Edge is in the care of the National Trust.

From the car park, walk across the grass to go through a gate and up some steps to a track. Turn left along this hedge-lined track, which heads gently uphill, by old quarry workings to the right, bending right and then left to reach a junction of tracks **A**.

Turn left and climb a stile beside a gate a few yards ahead to enter the woodlands of Blakeway Coppice, which clothe the steep sides of this section of Wenlock Edge. Follow a broad track for 50 yds (46m) to a footpath sign, here turning left up some steps, in the direction of Major's Leap, and soon bearing right to continue through this glorious woodland. The path keeps along the top of the ridge, above the huge deep gash of a quarry on the left, to reach Major's Leap, where a bench enables

you to enjoy in comfort the magnificent view over the wide and fertile Ape Dale below to Caer Caradoc, the Long Mynd and the Wrekin on the horizon. The name comes from the story that a local landowner and Royalist supporter, Major Smallman, was being pursued by Roundhead soldiers during the Civil War and rode his horse over the Edge to avoid capture. The horse was killed but the major's fall was broken by trees and he escaped.

From here turn left for a few yards and then right to continue above the quarry, by a wire fence on the left. Over to the left is a grand view of another group of Shropshire hills, this time the Clee Hills. At a barrier across the path and bridleway sign to Presthope **B**, bear right and head

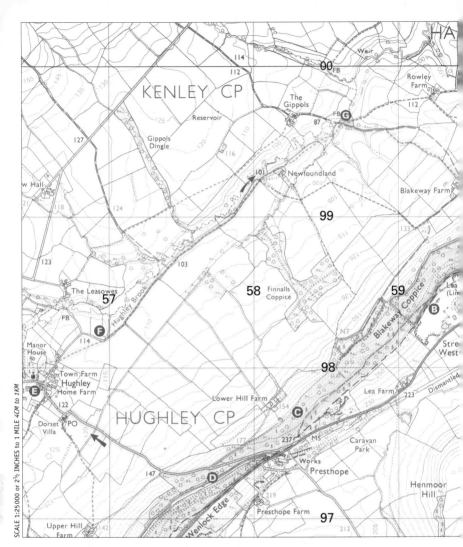

downhill to rejoin the broad track, bearing right along it. At a fork **C** take the right-hand downhill track, climb a stile beside a gate at the bottom edge of the woodland and bear left on joining another track. Follow the track to a lane **D** and turn right along it for ¾ mile (1.25km) into the village of Hughley.

In the village turn right beside the sturdy-looking 14th-century church **E** towards a modern bungalow, pass by a stable block, go through a metal gate and cross a field to a stile. Climb this, bear right across the next field, go through a metal gate and cross a track to climb another stile in front. Continue across the field corner, climb a stile, cross another track and climb another stile. Keep in the same direction across the next field, making for a hedge corner where a metal gate leads on to a track **F**.

Turn right along it – at first between hedges, later along the left-hand edge of fields, passing through several metal gates and keeping roughly parallel to the meandering Hughley Brook on the left. All the way along are fine views of the unmistakable Wrekin in front and the wooded Wenlock Edge on the right.

After passing to the left of an isolated house, do not bear left downhill to a gate and footbridge, but keep ahead in a

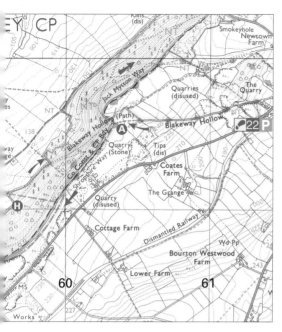

views through the trees, and soon the houses and church tower of Much Wenlock can be seen ahead. At a fork take the right-hand track between tall conifers, looking out for some steps on the right. Climb these, bear left at the top and continue along a path, passing through a wooden barrier to reach a junction of paths. Turn right through a gate and continue along the left-hand edge of a field – the bumps and hollows are the relics of now grassed over old quarries – keeping by a wire fence and woodland on the left, to a gate. Go through, continue by a hedge on the right to a marker-post and turn half-right, in the direction of Much Wenlock, passing to the left of a barn. Head across to another marker-post in a hedge gap and continue, by a hedge on the right, to reach a gate.

Go through and head downhill along the right-hand edge of a meadow, by a hedge on the left, continuing down to a stile. Climb it, turn left along a track for a few yards, turn right, then go down some steps and finally through a gate to return to the start. ●

straight line across a long tapering field, bearing slightly right to descend to a waymarked stile in the far right-hand corner. Climb the stile, cross the brook in front, bear left across a field towards trees and follow a path between them, by a brook on the left, descending into a hollow ⒢. Here cross a ditch and continue, keeping by a line of trees on the left, which curves to the right, to reach a gate at the top end of the field. Go through, keep along the right-hand edge of a field, by a hedge on the right, passing to the left of Blakeway Farm and going through a gate at the end of the field.

Cross a drive, climb a stile opposite and continue along an uphill tree-lined track to reach a clearing ⒣. Here bear left along the bottom edge of woodland and at a fork take the right-hand uphill path, between high banks, for a fairly steep but steady climb to regain the top of the Edge.

At the top the outward route is a few yards to the right ⒜, but turn sharply to the left along a track which heads downhill. From this track are more fine

Classic English landscape from Wenlock Edge

Castlemorton Common and the British Camp

Start	Car park below the British Camp – opposite the Malvern Hills Hotel on A449 about 3½ miles (5.6km) south of Great Malvern
Distance	7 miles (11.3km)
Approximate time	3½ hours
Parking	British Camp car park
Refreshments	Malvern Hills Hotel and refreshment kiosk at start, pub at Castlemorton
Ordnance Survey maps	Landranger 150 (Worcester & The Malverns), Explorer 14 (Malvern Hills)

As well as the dramatic and extensive views that inevitably accompany any walk on the Malvern Hills, this ramble in the southern part of the range embraces both a variety of terrain and considerable historic interest. It begins by descending from the slopes of the Herefordshire Beacon to the remains of Little Malvern Priory, and continues at the foot of the hills across the flat and open expanse of Castlemorton Common, a relic of the medieval hunting ground of Malvern Chase. After entering Eastnor Park to enjoy the fine view from the obelisk, you climb steadily to the summit of the Herefordshire Beacon, at 1114ft (340m) the second-highest point on the Malverns and the site of a large Iron Age fort, hence its alternative name of the British Camp.

Start by facing the Malvern Hills Hotel and turn sharp right to walk down to the lower and narrowing end of the car park. From here continue along a downhill tarmac track that curves to the left, passing to the left of a small reservoir and to the right of a house. Past the house this becomes a rough track that continues steeply downhill into woodland. At a fork, take the left-hand downhill path, by a stream on the right. Go through a metal gate and keep ahead across a field to climb a stile on to a farm drive.

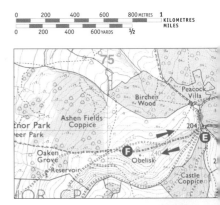

Turn left along the drive towards Little Malvern Priory, keeping to the left of the topiary hedge bordering Little Malvern Court, a large house which incorporates within its structure some of the domestic buildings of the priory. At the road turn right, passing the entrances to the Court and priory. In the Middle Ages Little Malvern Priory was one of the smallest Benedictine monasteries in the country; nowadays it is even smaller, comprising just the tower and east end of the church, which dates from a late 15th- and early 16th-century rebuilding. Nevertheless this is a delightful building, which is enhanced by its setting at the foot of the thickly wooded hills.

Turn right over a stile beside a metal gate, at a footpath sign **A**, and head diagonally across a field – there is no visible path – to a waymarked stile. Climb this, continue across the next field to climb another stile and keep across the next field for about 50 yds (46m), climbing a stile by a hedge corner. Passing to the left of a house, go through a gate and along a tree-lined track to a lane.

Turn right along the lane, passing through a metal gate and continuing across the rough grass and gorse and through the scattered trees of Castlemorton Common, one of several areas of common lying below the Malverns. Despite being crossed by roads,

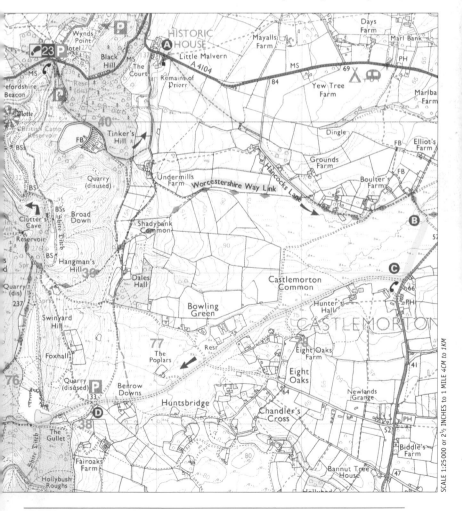

SCALE 1:25000 or 2½ INCHES to 1 MILE 4CM to 1KM

it still retains something of the appearance and atmosphere of the medieval chase. Malvern Chase was originally a royal forest, covering a large area to the east of the hills, but was given by Edward I to the powerful Gilbert de Clare, Earl of Gloucester, when the latter married the King's daughter in 1290.

After crossing a stream, the tarmac lane becomes a rough track which bends to the left and continues to a T-junction. Turn right, almost immediately curving left to cross a stream **B** and then turn half-right to strike out across the rough common in the direction of the houses of Castlemorton, aiming to reach the road near a junction. A pub is about 100 yds (91m) ahead, but the route turns right at the junction **C** along a narrow unfenced lane to continue across the common. In front is a view of the line of the Malverns.

After nearly $1\frac{1}{2}$ miles (2.4km), you ascend gently to a junction of roads and tracks **D**, where you keep straight ahead along a tarmac track, making for a gap in the hills. The tarmac track ends at the car park below the disused Gullet Quarry. This was the last working quarry in the Malverns, closed in the 1970s and made into an attractive site by the Malvern Hills Conservators. Continue along a path, passing to the left of a pool below the quarry, to join a track. Bear right along this track, which heads uphill through a delightful wooded valley, below the slopes of Midsummer Hill on the left, to reach a junction of tracks just in front of the boundary fence of Eastnor Park **E**.

The route continues to the right, but it is worthwhile to make a short diversion here, going through a gate into the park. Take the uphill track straight ahead to the obelisk **F**, a memorial to the Somers family of Eastnor Castle, in order to enjoy the magnificent all-round view that includes the Gothic pile of Eastnor Castle below, built in the early 19th century in imitation of a medieval fortress.

Retrace your steps to go through the park gate **E** and turn left to rejoin the main route, heading uphill along a track through splendid woodland. On emerging into slightly more open country, bear right, off the track, on to a narrow path which keeps parallel and above it for a while, before bearing right to head up to the ridge. Here turn left on to a broad track which keeps along the ridge and from now on come magnificent views, over both sides and ahead, virtually all the way. At a stone, inscribed 'Hangman's Hill and Broad Down', continue along the track to the left and keep on the main track all the while to pass in front of Clutter's (or Giant's) Cave, allegedly named after an 18th-century occupant who, from the size of the cave, was certainly no giant. Continue past the cave to climb to a circular direction stone, one of several erected by the Malvern Hills Conservators and most useful to walkers.

Here turn left in the 'British Camp' direction and head steeply uphill along a recently constructed stone path, passing through the outer ramparts of the Iron Age fort. Bear right across an open grassy area and continue through the complex earthworks to climb to the top of the Herefordshire Beacon. The British Camp is one of the largest and most impressive Iron Age forts in the country, with high banks and deep ditches; the outer ramparts are $1\frac{1}{4}$ miles (2km) in circumference, the fort covered an area of about 30 acres and, it has been estimated, could house 20,000 people. From the summit, an often breezy spot 1114ft (340m) high, the views over Herefordshire, the northern hills of the Malverns and across the Vale of Severn to the Cotswolds are truly magnificent, described by the 17th-century writer Evelyn as the 'goodliest in England'.

From here a broad, well-constructed, partially stepped path leads downhill to the car park and starting point. ●

Stiperstones

Start	Car park off minor road between [...] about 1½ miles (2.4km) north-we[...]
Distance	7 miles (11.3km)
Approximate time	3½ hours
Parking	Stiperstones car park
Refreshments	None
Ordnance Survey maps	Landranger 137 (Ludlow & Wenlock Edge) and Pathfinder 909, SO 29/39 (Montgomery)

The sombre and forbidding-looking ridge of the Stiperstones, 1731ft (528m) at the highest point, is unlike any of the other Shropshire hills. The succession of serrated quartzite rock pinnacles that punctuate the ridge give it an appearance more reminiscent of the wilder parts of Dartmoor or the Pennines, and there is a definite feeling of remoteness and loneliness in this thinly populated area. Walking on the rocky ridge itself requires some care, but otherwise the terrain is not difficult, the route is well waymarked, there are just a few modest climbs, and the views over Shropshire and the Welsh border country are superb.

Turn right out of the car park, walk along the lane for ½ mile (800m) to a T-junction, turn right and, at a public footpath sign about 50 yds (46m) ahead, turn left over a stile **A**. Bearing right, head across the corner of a field to a stile, climb it and continue across a rough and uneven gorse-strewn field, heading downhill to climb a stile to the left of the old mine workings of the Bog. It was the Romans who began the mining of zinc and lead in this area, which continued until the 1950s.

Go down steps and keep ahead, winding between bushes and bracken, and passing to the left of a pool – there are spoil heaps and some ruined mine buildings nearby – to rejoin the lane just to the left of a bend **B**.

Turn left and, where the lane bends to the right by Stiperstones Field Centre,

keep ahead, at a public footpath sign, along a broad straight track. Keep ahead again where the track forks, cross a brook and climb a stile beside a gate. Continue along the track, between a hedge on the right and the edge of a conifer plantation on the left, watching for a stile on the right just beyond a metal gate. Climb this, bear left and head across a succession of fields, keeping in the same direction all the time and climbing a series of waymarked stiles. After climbing the fourth stile, continue across rough grass to cross a brook, keep ahead for another 100 yds (91m) and, just after passing the second waymark, bear left across a large open field. Climb two stiles to the left of two metal gates (in quick succession) and continue, at first climbing gently – soon Shelve Pool is seen ahead – later heading down to a stile. Climb this stile and a

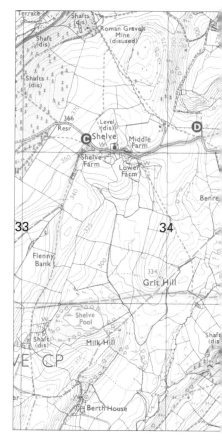

and keep ahead, crossing a ..., climbing a third stile in the field ...er and continuing towards the group ...trees beside Shelve Pool.

Walk along the edge of the trees, passing to the right of the pool, and head uphill, by a wire fence on the right, to climb a stile. Bear right and continue uphill across a field, looking out for a stile in the top right-hand corner. Climb this stile, keep ahead to climb a second, and a third about 50 yds (46m) in front, and continue, passing through a metal gate. Now keep by a wire fence and conifer plantation on the right and, after both fence and plantation end, continue straight ahead across grass to a metal gate. Go through this and through another gate to join a track and follow it up to a road **C**.

Turn right through the isolated hamlet of Shelve, passing to the right of the plain and sturdy-looking 19th-century church which needs to be robust as it occupies a windswept spot over 1100ft (335m) high. After ¹/₂ mile (800m) the road bends sharply to the right; here climb a stile, at a public footpath sign **D** and head uphill across a field, joining and keeping by a wire fence on the left. Turn left over a stile

The shattered rocks of the Stiperstones ridge

in that fence and bear right to head across a large field, going through a waymarked metal gate and continuing across the next field to a fence corner. Here bear right – fine views all around – to climb a stile and bear right again, heading slightly uphill

SCALE 1:25 000 or 2½ INCHES to 1 MILE 4CM to 1KM

across rough pasture towards a circle of pine trees. Keeping by a hedge on the right, turn right over a stile and continue along the right-hand edge of a field, by a hedge and wire fence on the right. On meeting a farm track, turn left and head downhill. Go through a metal gate and, at a T-junction, turn left again along a track which bears right to reach a lane.

Turn left and after 50 yds (46m) turn right along an uphill, hedge-lined track **E**, passing to the left of more lead-mine workings. In front of a Methodist Chapel (dated 1869), bear left to continue steadily uphill, bear left again at a T-junction and now comes an impressive view ahead of the Stiperstones ridge, dominated by the jagged outcrop of the Devil's Chair. Continue to a gate and stile which give access to the Stiperstones National Nature Reserve. Climb the stile and follow the broad track ahead, between gorse and heather, across a lovely wild and open landscape, with grand views down a steep-sided valley to the left and of the serrated ridge in front.

Head steadily uphill towards the ridge and, at a crossroads just to the right of the outcrop of Shepherd's Rock **F**, turn right along the very rocky ridge path up to the Devil's Chair, the most prominent of the groups of rocks on the Stiperstones ridge. From here the views are magnificent. Follow the path through the massive shattered rocks, continue past Manstone Rock – where there is a triangulation pillar – and other outcrops to where the path divides. Here take the left fork and follow a broad, pleasant, grassy path gently downhill to climb a stile to enter the car park. ●

Shakespeare Country

Start	Stratford-upon-Avon
Distance	10 miles (16km)
Approximate time	5 hours
Parking	Stratford-upon-Avon
Refreshments	Restaurants, pubs and cafés at Stratford-upon-Avon, pub and cafés at Shottery, pubs at Welford-on-Avon
Ordnance Survey maps	Landranger 151 (Stratford-upon-Avon), Pathfinders 997, SP 05/15 (Stratford-upon-Avon (West) & Alcester) and 998, SP 25/35 (Stratford-upon-Avon (East))

This lengthy but easy-paced walk in the heart of Shakespeare Country may well include paths used by the Bard himself. It is memorable for a number of reasons. As well as the Shakespearean connections at Stratford and Shottery, there are the villages of black-and-white half-timbered Tudor cottages and medieval churches, and a tranquil countryside of wide views and attractive riverside scenery. From Stratford the route first proceeds to Anne Hathaway's Cottage at Shottery and continues across fields to Binton, before descending to cross the river at the delightful village of Welford. Then comes a short walk to Weston before the grand finale – a glorious 3-mile (4.8km) ramble by the banks of Shakespeare's Avon back to Stratford.

Even if Shakespeare had not been born here, Stratford's wealth of half-timbered Tudor buildings and attractive riverside location would still make it a major tourist attraction. But you can never escape the fact that he was born here: Shakespeare's influence permeates the whole town and has made it one of the world's great centres of literary pilgrimage. Throughout Stratford are various buildings and monuments that illustrate almost all the stages in Shakespeare's life, and more especially the huge industry that has grown up in the centuries following his death. There is his father's prosperous 16th-century house, where Shakespeare was born in 1564; the

Grammar School and adjoining 15th-century Guild Chapel, where he went to school; the 15th-century Clopton Bridge he crossed on his way to London; the foundations and gardens of New Place, where he lived during the latter part of his life and where he died; the splendid half-timbered Hall's Croft, where his daughter Susanna and her husband lived; and the medieval Holy Trinity Church, by the river, in which he is buried. More recent are the 19th-century statue of him in the riverside gardens and the Royal Shakespeare Theatre, rebuilt in 1932 after fire destroyed its Victorian predecessor.

The walk starts at Shakespeare's statue. Walk across the riverside gardens towards the Royal Shakespeare Theatre, passing to the right of it, and turn right along Chapel Lane. By the Guild Chapel, turn left into Church Street, continue to the end and turn right along Chestnut Walk to a road junction. Here cross two converging roads and take the tarmac path ahead, signposted 'Anne Hathaway's Cottage' **A**. This first part of the walk may well follow the route that Shakespeare used to take across the fields to Shottery, but the fields are now a recreation ground and the modern growth of Stratford has almost engulfed Shottery and turned it into a virtual suburb.

The path keeps in a straight line between garden walls and fences, crossing several roads before continuing across a recreation ground. At a fork, take the right-hand path, passing to the right of school buildings, and continue, bearing left at the next fork – signposted 'Anne Hathaway's Cottage via Shottery' into Shottery village. Turn right along Tavern Lane, following it around a left-hand bend to a road. Keep ahead to a crossroads and here there is a choice: either continue ahead along Cottage Lane, or (a pleasant alternative) take the Jubilee Walk – created to commemorate the Queen's Silver Jubilee in 1977 – a path which runs parallel to and above the road on the right, turning left over Shottery Brook to rejoin the road opposite Anne Hathaway's Cottage **B**.

This half-timbered thatched farmhouse must be one of the most photographed buildings in the country. Anne Hathaway was eight years older than Shakespeare and they were married in 1582, when he was 18 and she was 26. The colourful Tudor garden in front and the secluded orchard beyond enhance the overall attractiveness of the scene.

Turn right along the road, soon passing Shottery Hamlet, another picturesque group of thatched black-and-white cottages. Where the road turns right, turn

left and then almost immediately right, along Hathaway Green Lane through a modern housing area. At the first crossroads turn left, follow the road as it curves to the right, and by a public footpath sign to Drayton **C** turn left over a stile and keep in a straight line across the large field ahead. Continue across the next field, keeping parallel to and to the right of a line of telegraph poles, to a stile. Climb this, keep ahead to climb another and continue along the right-hand edge of the next field. Go through a metal gate, keep ahead, passing to the left of farm buildings, and go through a hedge gap to continue by a wire fence and line of trees on the right.

After about 50 yds (46m) turn right over one stile, climb another in front and bear slightly left to follow the direction of a waymark along a faint path across a field to the far end, where the field tapers. Here bear right through a metal gate, cross a brook, go through another metal gate ahead and continue along the left-hand side of a field, by the brook and a line of trees on the left. Climb two stiles in quick succession and continue in the same direction across the next field. Go through a metal gate and keep ahead, looking out for a waymarked stile on the right about 50 yds (46m) before the end of the field. Climb this, turn left along the field edge, following it around to the right, and at the far end turn right again, turning left through a hedge gap at a waymark. Continue along a track by the right-hand edge of the next field, following as it curves first to the right and, at a waymark a few yards ahead, to the left. Keeping to the right of farm buildings, follow the track through two metal gates to a lane.

Turn right and follow the lane as it bends left into Binton. Just before the Victorian church, turn left over a waymarked stile **D** and head gently downhill along the left-hand edge of a field, by a hedge on the left. Climb a stile

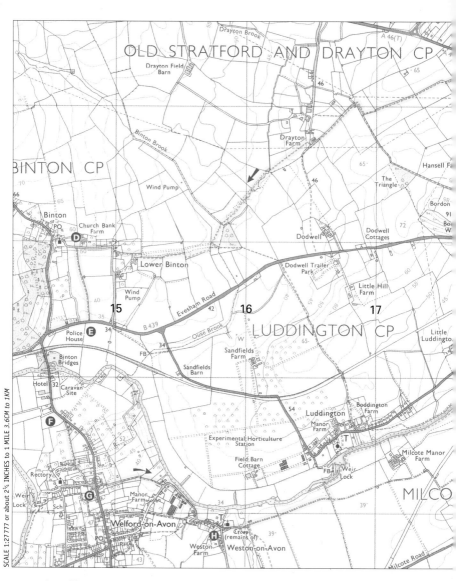

SCALE 1:27777 or about 2¼ INCHES to 1 MILE 3.6CM to 1KM

0 200 400 600 800 METRES 1
0 200 400 600 YARDS ½
KILOMETRES
MILES

on to a road **E**, turn right along this busy road for ¼ mile (400m) and take the first turning on the left – signposted to Welford and Long Marston – to cross the River Avon. Continue into Welford and, just after the road curves left, bear right, by a half-hidden footpath sign **F**, on to a narrow hedge-lined path – which later keeps along the left-hand side of fields – to reach a stile. Climb this, cross a lane and bear left to continue along a tarmac

hedge-lined path, going through a metal kissing-gate and keeping ahead to a lane in the centre of Welford-on-Avon, an idyllic village. To the right, a street of thatched half-timbered cottages leads to the medieval church, which boasts a 12th-century Norman nave, 14th-century chancel and 15th-century west tower.

The route continues to the left to the village green **G**; crossing the road here and taking the waymarked path opposite. Follow it between hedges – later between wire fences – to some houses, keep ahead along a drive and shortly bear left to walk

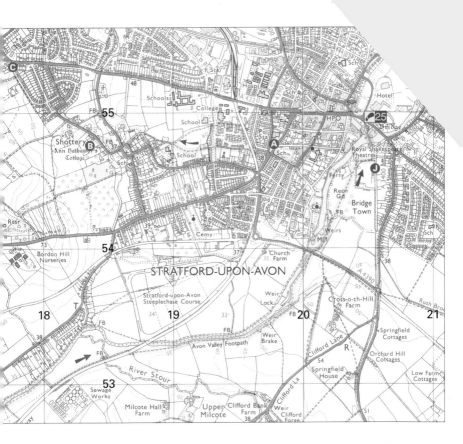

along a parallel path to a T-junction. Here follow a yellow waymark to the left along a tarmac drive and, after passing a thatched house on the left, continue along a hedge-lined track with the river below.

The track curves gradually to the right and keeps by the river, before heading gently uphill away from it into Weston-on-Avon, a smaller and quieter village than Welford but with more black-and-white thatched cottages and a small 15th-century church. On reaching a lane turn left and, where the lane bears right **H**, bear left along a track, passing to the right of the church. Keep in a straight line along this track, first between fields and later across them, following the regular waymarks until one of these directs you to turn left to the riverbank.

Turn right at the river to follow the riverside path for 3 miles (4.8km) back to Stratford – a superb finale to this walk. The route is well waymarked and easy to follow, keeps by the river for most of the way, goes through a series of gates and over stiles, and traverses lush tree-fringed meadows. The only time you leave the river is where a waymark directs you first to the right, then to the left along the edge of a field below the embankment of a disused railway to cross a footbridge over the River Stour, after which you pass under a disused railway bridge, soon to rejoin the Avon. The spire of Holy Trinity Church is in sight for most of the time.

On approaching Stratford, the path climbs above the wooded riverside bank before passing under a bridge and along the edge of a recreation ground, with views across the river to Holy Trinity Church and later the Royal Shakespeare Theatre. Finally, just before the road, turn left over the early 19th-century Tramway Bridge **J**, built for the horse-drawn Stratford to Moreton-in-Marsh Railway, to return to the Shakespeare statue. ●

Brown Clee Hill

Start	Parking area on minor road between Stoke St Milborough and Clee St Margaret, about ¾ mile (1.25km) north of Stoke St Milborough
Distance	7½ miles (12.1km)
Approximate time	3½ hours
Parking	Parking area at side of road
Refreshments	None
Ordnance Survey maps	Landranger 137 (Ludlow & Wenlock Edge) and Pathfinder 931, SO 48/58 (Craven Arms)

The Clee Hills lie between Bridgnorth and Ludlow, rising to the twin summits of Brown Clee Hill and Titterstone Clee Hill, both of which are occupied by radio masts. This walk climbs to Abdon Burf, the summit of Brown Clee Hill which, at 1771ft (540m), is not only the highest point in Shropshire but the highest point anywhere in the Heart of England. Although the ascents and descents are gradual and easy, there is some rough and boggy terrain near the tops, and this is a walk best done on a fine day, as in misty weather there are places where route finding could be difficult, unless you are experienced in the use of a compass. Much of the walk is across a working, private common (Clee Liberty), owned by Clee St Margaret Parish Meeting. This land is not a right of way and walkers enter it with the permission of the landowners. Please respect this privilege and follow the Country Code at all times. *Throughout the walk the extensive views over the surrounding hills of Shropshire and Worcestershire are magnificent.*

Begin by climbing a stile at the side of the parking area and walk gently uphill along the right-hand edge of open grassland, by a hedge-bank on the right. Immediately there is a fine view of Brown Clee Hill ahead, and soon an equally good view of Titterstone Clee Hill to the right. Keep by the hedge-bank and later a wire fence on the right all the time, walking on pleasant, springy and short-cropped turf. Just after passing a house on the left, the wire fence bears to the right but you keep ahead,

following a grassy path between bracken and gorse and heading steadily uphill across rough moorland more or less in a straight line. After a while the exact line of route becomes less obvious – there are several grassy alternatives – but continue in the same north-easterly direction to reach a rough stony track **A**. To the left is a good view of the prominent earthworks of Nordy Bank Fort.

Bear right along the winding uphill track for ¼ mile (400m). Shortly after

ABDON CP
Fair View
87
Bank House
Marsh Farm
Overdale
Abdon Bridge
Abdon Marsh
Medieval Village of Abdon (site of)
Abdon
FB
Ford
Manor House
New House
Spr
Wireless Station
Abdon Burf
Masts
Spring Cottage
Abdon Liberty
Quarry House
86
Allpike
Council Cottages
Sandy Nap
57
Brookfield
58
Prospect House
59
Highcroft
Monkeys' Fold
The Five Springs
Woodbank
Upper House
Coneybury
Lower Cross Lanes
The Plough
Cockshutford
Pole Gutter Cottage
Brown Clee Hill
85
Cleemarsh
The Orchard
Nordy Bank Fort
Clee Liberty
New House Farm
CLEE ST MARGARET CP
Quarry (dis)
Navigational Relay Station
Castle Covert
Clee Burf Settlement
The Green Shutters
The Sands
Upper Hill House
The Yeld
84
Thornwell
Reservoir
Stoke Enclosure
The Toot
Stokegorse
26
Bockleton Court
0 200 400 600 800 METRES 1 KILOMETRES
0 200 400 600 YARDS ½ MILES

SCALE 1:25 000 or 2½ INCHES to 1 MILE *4CM to 1KM*

crossing a small stream the track curves right to head up to the radio station on Clee Burf, the second highest point on Brown Clee Hill. Here keep straight ahead along a reasonably discernible grassy path which initially keeps parallel to and below the track on the right, later passing between low embankments and continuing across the shoulder of the hill. Ahead is a fine view of Abdon Burf. The path levels off for a while before continuing upwards and finally, on approaching woodland in front, bears slightly left to arrive at the hollow that lies between Clee Burf and Abdon Burf.

Brown Clee Hill, the highest point in Shropshire

At a Shropshire Way sign go through a metal gate **B** and continue uphill, between heather, along a straight and clear track, later joining and keeping by a wire fence on the left. On reaching a crossroads of tracks **C**, turn right and head across rough terrain to the triangulation pillar by the radio masts on the summit of Abdon Burf. From here there is an extensive panoramic view that includes the Abberley Hills, the Malverns, Bringewood Chase, Long Mynd, Wenlock Edge and the Wrekin.

Retrace your steps to the crossroads of tracks by the fence **C** and keep ahead through a gap in the fence to head downhill, by a wire fence on the left. On reaching another fence ahead – by a metal gate on the left – turn right and continue downhill along a pleasant grassy sunken track, passing through one metal gate and on down to another. Go through that on to a lane, continue downhill along the lane to a T-junction and turn left, in the direction of Abdon and Tugford. After about 50 yds (46m), turn left over a stile **D** beside a metal gate and walk along the left-hand edge of a field, by a wire fence on the left. Climb a stile and keep ahead downhill, over two stiles in quick succession at the bottom, narrow end of the field, and continue along a sunken, tree-lined and likely to be muddy path down to another stile.

Climb that, keep ahead to cross a plank over a brook, pass in front of a house and go through a gate to continue along a tree-lined track, reaching a lane in front of farm buildings **E**. Turn left along this quiet narrow lane for 1 mile (1.6km) to a crossroads **F**, here turning left along another narrow lane, signposted to Cockshutford, for another ¹/₂ mile (800m).

Where the lane curves to the left **G**, keep ahead through a metal gate – at a notice: 'No Vehicles Allowed, Footpath Only' – and along a track, to go through an identical gate. Continue on a steadily ascending track, passing to the left of the earthworks of Nordy Bank Fort, the best-preserved of the various prehistoric forts on the Clee Hills. Ahead and to the left is a grand view of the long ridge of Brown Clee Hill. Just after the track bears left to continue in a straight line towards Clee Burf, turn right along a grassy track – there are a number of green tracks at this stage, but bear right all the while, making towards the group of trees ahead.

Pass to the right of this group of trees and continue downhill to join a hedge-bank on the left. Here you rejoin the outward route to retrace your steps to the starting point.

Much Wenlock, Ironbridge Gorge and Buildwas Park

Start	Much Wenlock
Distance	11½ miles (18.5km)
Approximate time	6 hours
Parking	Much Wenlock
Refreshments	Pubs and cafés at Much Wenlock, pubs and cafés at Ironbridge
Ordnance Survey maps	Landranger 127 (Stafford & Telford), Pathfinders 890, SJ 60/70 (Iron-Bridge & Telford (South)) and 911, SO 69/79 (Bridgnorth & Much Wenlock)

A well-waymarked route across fields and through woodlands takes you from the quiet countryside around Much Wenlock, with its mellowed monastic ruins, to the totally different environment of the Ironbridge Gorge, with its dramatic steep-sided and thickly wooded hillsides, early industrial monuments and modern power station. After crossing the renowned iron bridge, you follow a fascinating walk through the gorge by the River Severn, before reaching more medieval monastic remains and a return to more tranquil surroundings and gentler scenery. It would be difficult to conceive of a walk offering greater scenic and historic contrasts and, although lengthy, it is neither difficult nor strenuous.

Much Wenlock, which lies at the north-eastern end of Wenlock Edge, is an attractive old town of stone houses and cottages, with a rare surviving example of a town farm, a medieval timbered Guildhall and a fine 12th-century church. The impressive remains of Wenlock Priory belong to a Cluniac house founded by Roger of Montgomery, the powerful Earl of Shrewsbury, soon after the Norman Conquest. Part of the south side of the nave and south transept of the church survive, dating from the 13th century, and the chapter house is noted for its intricate carvings. Much of the eastern range of the cloisters was rebuilt and extended in the late 15th century and this was converted into a private residence after Henry VIII's dissolution of the monasteries.

Start in the town centre, walk past the Guildhall and parish church, and turn first right along the Bull Ring, passing the priory ruins. Keep along the lane for just over ½ mile (800m), following it around a sharp right-hand bend; later the lane becomes a rough track. The first part of the walk, between Much Wenlock and Ironbridge, follows the Shropshire Way.

Climb a stone stile beside a gate, continue, passing to the right of a farm, and keep by the wall of the farmhouse to climb a stile and cross a footbridge. Turn left and head across a field, bearing gradually away from the stream on the

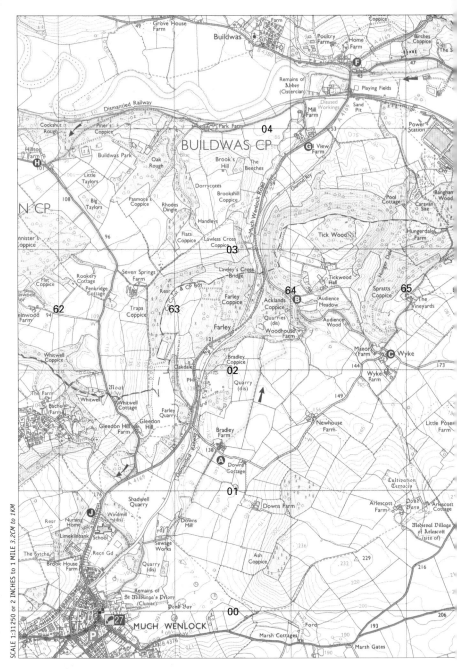

left and looking out for a waymarked stile in front. Climb this, keep along the left-hand edge of the next field, climb another stile and continue along a farm track. Where the track ends, climb a stile, cross a lane **Ⓐ** and go through a metal gate into a farmyard, following a yellow waymark to the left to pass through another metal gate. Bear right between the buildings of Bradley Farm, go through a metal gate in front and turn half-left to head diagonally across a large field, making for a hedge on the far side and turning left to keep by the hedge to a stile in the field corner.

Climb it, continue along the right-hand edge of the next field, by a hedge on the

```
0    200   400   600   800 METRES 1
|----|----|----|----|----| KILOMETRES
0    200   400   600 YARDS  1/2     MILES
```

confusing; several paths come to a dead end and there are some dangerous sections along the edges of disused quarries – therefore follow the route directions through the wood carefully.

Follow the path ahead through this most attractive woodland and, on meeting a track at a U-bend, take the right-hand fork. The track bears to the right and you pass beside a metal gate; a few yards further on turn very sharply to the left, at a yellow waymark and Shropshire Way sign, along another track which soon curves to the right to keep along the edge of the wood high above the Ironbridge Gorge. Continue as far as a cottage, here turning left and taking the left-hand path at a fork. The path soon turns right and heads downhill to join a track. From here the view through the trees of the towers of the power station looks strangely romantic; enhanced by their pink colour and with the Wrekin as a backcloth. Bear right along the track, taking care to keep left at a fork to continue along a narrower path down into a gully. Head up again and continue to the top of some steps. Turn left down the steps, turn right along a path, then sharp left down more steps, heading directly towards the cooling towers and continuing downhill by a fence on the right. Go down more steps, bearing right near the bottom and on down to a crossing of paths.

Turn right along a wooded path with the River Severn below on the left, go down more steps and, at the bottom of these, turn left to join a disused railway track. Turn right along this and just before a bridge, bear left through a gap and keep ahead to climb a stile. A short distance ahead turn left **D** to cross the Severn by the iron bridge and enter the town of the same name.

This, the world's first iron bridge, is the focal point of a whole series of early industrial monuments in the area which claims to be the 'birthplace of the

right but, where the field edge curves slightly to the left, look out for a yellow waymarked gate on the right. Go through it: at this point the right of way continues ahead across the middle of the field, shortly turning left to rejoin the field edge and turning right along it, but walkers will find it easier to turn left by the field edge, following it around to the right and along to the far end of the field. Here go through a metal gate, continue along a track, passing to the right of a farm house, and follow this winding downhill track through woodland to reach a lane **B**.

Turn right along the lane for just over $^1/_2$ mile (800m) into the hamlet of Wyke, where the lane turns first to the left and after a few yards to the right **C**. At this point continue straight ahead along a downhill track, over a stream in the valley bottom and uphill to where the track turns left to a house. Here keep ahead to climb a waymarked stile, continue by a wire fence on the left and go through a hedge gap. Now keep along the left-hand edge of the next field, and climb another stile to enter Benthall Edge Wood. There are many paths and different waymarked trails through this wood which can be

Industrial Revolution'. Ample supplies of timber, together with local sources of limestone, coal and iron, made this part of Shropshire an early centre of the iron industry. In 1709 Abraham Darby first smelted iron ore with coke instead of charcoal at his Coalbrookdale works, an event which revolutionised the industry by freeing it from its dependence on timber, which was now becoming scarce, and thus enabling it to expand. This also caused the Ironbridge area to become a major iron-producing region and led to demands for a new bridge across the Severn gorge. The bridge was completed in 1779, a most impressive structure and regarded as the wonder of the age.

After crossing the bridge turn left along the road through the gorge for ½ mile (800m) and, at the Museum of the River Visitor Centre, a 19th-century Gothic building that was formerly a warehouse for the Coalbrookdale Company **E**, turn left down some steps to the river. Now turn right along a riverside path, passing through a park – where the path becomes a broad tarmac drive – and, where this drive bears right, keep ahead, at a blue waymark, along a path through a meadow and picnic area, with the power station on the other side of the river.

Pass under Albert Edward Bridge – built by the Coalbrookdale Company in 1863 – keeping by the river all the time. Although the path is paved in places, there are parts where it is quite slippery, and care is needed as it is very close to the river; barriers have been erected at intervals. Pass under a second bridge, continue under a third and shortly afterwards the road and river are so close that you must climb a fence on to the road for a short distance, reclimbing the fence when a narrow and faint path appears on the left. (The next section is quite overgrown and may be boggy, so some walkers may prefer to stay on the road up to Buildwas Bridge, rejoining the route at **F** below.)

After passing under the next bridge, go through a metal gate to join an easier stretch across meadowland. At the end of a tapering riverside meadow, bear right to climb a stile beside a metal gate and, turning left, rejoin the road **F**. Turn left again over Buildwas Bridge. To the right, you pass the drive leading down to Buildwas Abbey, which lies in a quiet and secluded position near the Severn. This was a small Cistercian monastery. The surviving buildings are mostly of the 12th century and the church is almost intact, a superb example of the Transitional style.

Continue along the road for ¼ mile (400m) and, at a group of farm buildings **G**, turn right down a clearly defined tarmac track, from which there are attractive views of the abbey to the right. The track bends sharply to the left and continues between hedges. After passing farm buildings and houses, it becomes a pleasant grassy track which continues through the woodlands of Buildwas Park. Eventually go through a metal gate to the right of a house and bear right along a tarmac drive to a lane **H**.

Turn left along this quiet and undulating lane, and after 1½ miles (2.4km) it ascends, between trees, to a fork where you bear right to a road. Turn right into Much Wenlock and, opposite a row of houses – just before reaching school buildings on the left – turn left through a gate **J** and follow a distinct path along the right-hand edge of a sloping field, by a hedge, line of trees and wire fence on the right. Passing to the left of the school buildings, keep along this attractive path to go through a metal gate into woodland. Shortly afterwards turn right through a kissing-gate into a recreation ground and follow a path, lined by tall trees, along the edge of it, going through a gate at the far end on to a road.

Keep ahead to a junction, turn left into the centre of Much Wenlock, turning right by the church to return to the start. ●

The Long Mynd

Start	Church Stretton
Distance	8 miles (12.9km)
Approximate time	4 hours
Parking	Church Stretton
Refreshments	Pubs and cafés at Church Stretton, National Trust café at Carding Mill Valley, pub at Little Stretton
Ordnance Survey maps	Landranger 137 (Ludlow & Wenlock Edge) and Pathfinder 910, SO 49/59 (Church Stretton)

The Long Mynd is the prominent whale-backed hill that rises abruptly above the western side of the Onny valley between Church Stretton and Craven Arms, looking out over the Welsh border country. Indeed the word 'mynd' is Welsh for mountain. On its eastern side it is cut into by a number of narrow valleys, locally called 'batches', and the walk begins by ascending one of these, the well-known Carding Mill Valley, to reach the ridge. Then follows a superlative ridgetop walk, with magnificent views on both sides, passing the highest point on the Long Mynd before descending back into the valley and returning to the start. Most of this spectacular and quite energetic walk is on National Trust land.

The pleasant little town of Church Stretton, lying at the foot of the Long Mynd, has all the ingredients that make up an excellent walking centre: cradled by hills and at the hub of a network of footpaths, with good communications by both road and rail, parking facilities and a number of hotels and guest houses, pubs and teashops. It has an agreeably old-fashioned air, as befits a town that became a health resort in the late Victorian era, but its main building is much older – a fine parish church which dates back to the Norman period.

The walk begins in the Square, off the High Street. Head northwards along the High Street and, at a crossroads, turn left along Burway Road, soon bearing right and following signs for the Burway and

Long Mynd. The narrow lane heads steadily uphill for nearly ½ mile (800m), crossing a cattle-grid to enter the National Trust property of Long Mynd **A**.

Here bear slightly right on to a track that heads along the side of the beautiful, steep-sided, gorse-, bracken- and heather-covered slopes of the Carding Mill Valley, with a stream below on the right. Ahead are fine views looking towards the head of the valley, which gets its name from the carding process, by which wool was 'carded' or combed prior to spinning. The track descends to the stream and joins a road; follow the road through the valley, passing by buildings that now belong to the National Trust, which include a gift shop and café. Turn right over a footbridge, turn left along a track – now the stream is on your left – soon rejoining the road, and continue along this as it climbs gently to reach a car park.

Bear slightly left to cross a footbridge and continue along a track, with the stream on the right, still climbing gently. Where the valley divides, bear right to cross the stream and continue uphill through the narrow, secluded right-hand valley, across heathery expanses and still with a stream on your right, eventually to reach the top of the broad ridge at a footpath sign and junction of tracks. Keep ahead for a few yards and then turn left **B** on to the track that runs along the top of the Long Mynd, giving superb views in all directions.

Continue along this main track – there are at this point several parallel tracks – and at a junction of tracks keep straight ahead along a narrower track, passing to the left of a shooting-box to reach a lane **C**. Cross over and continue along the track ahead, crossing another track and heading up through heather to the triangulation pillar and toposcope on Pole Bank, at 1693ft (516m), the highest point on the Long Mynd. As might be expected, the all-round views over the Shropshire hills and Welsh borders are magnificent, and the toposcope shows that, in clear conditions, Cadair Idris and the Brecon Beacons can be seen, as well as closer features, including the Stiperstones, the hills of central Wales, Ragleth Hill, Caer Caradoc, the Clee Hills and Wenlock Edge.

Keep ahead past the triangulation pillar, descending gently to a lane and turn right along it to follow the line of a medieval trackway called the Port Way. Soon you pass a rare group of trees on the right and shortly afterwards, at a footpath sign to Little Stretton, turn left along a broad track **D**.

At a junction bear slightly left along a path through heather which keeps above the side of, and with views to the left over Ashes Hollow, one of the most beautiful of

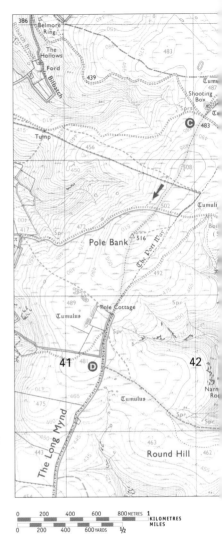

the 'batches' that cut into the flanks of the Long Mynd. The path later broadens into a track, heads downhill into an open grassy area called Barrister's Plain and then climbs again over the hill in front, passing to the left of a small isolated group of trees. Keep along this attractive green track high above Callow Hollow on the right, continuing over the shoulder of another hill (Callow) above the right-hand side of the valley of Small Batch on the left. Ahead there is a glorious view across the Onny valley, overshadowed by Ragleth Hill, with the village of Little Stretton below and Wenlock Edge beyond.

The track descends gently, joining and keeping by a wire fence on the right. Later it bears slightly left away from the fence and descends more steeply to a stream. Go through a gate and keep ahead, walking along the right-hand side of the stream, and then crossing it to reach a track. Continue past cottages on the left, cross a footbridge and then turn right into Little Stretton, taking the first turning on the left to a T-junction **E**. Opposite is Little Stretton's unusual black-and-white wooden thatched church.

At the T-junction turn left along the road for 1½ miles (2.4km) back to Church Stretton; a pleasant and generally quiet road with a footpath on the right for most of the way.

Further Information

 ## The National Trust

Anyone who likes visiting places of natural beauty and/or historic interest has cause to be grateful to the National Trust. Without it, many such places would probably have vanished by now.

It was in response to the pressures on the countryside posed by the relentless march of Victorian industrialisation that the trust was set up in 1895. Its founders, inspired by the common goals of protecting and conserving Britain's national heritage and widening public access to it, were Sir Robert Hunter, Octavia Hill and Canon Rawnsley: respectively a solicitor, a social reformer and a clergyman. The latter was particularly influential. As a canon of Carlisle Cathedral and vicar of Crosthwaite (near Keswick), he was concerned about threats to the Lake District and had already been active in protecting footpaths and promoting public access to open countryside. After the flooding of Thirlmere in 1879 to create a large reservoir, he became increasingly convinced that the only effective way to guarantee protection was outright ownership of land.

The purpose of the National Trust is to preserve areas of natural beauty and sites of historic interest by acquisition, holding them in trust for the nation and making them available for public access and enjoyment. Some of its properties have been acquired through purchase, but many have been donated. Nowadays the National Trust is not only one of the biggest landowners in the country, but also one of the most active conservation charities, protecting 581,113 acres (253,176 ha) of land, including 555 miles (892km) of coastline, and over 300 historic properties in England, Wales and Northern Ireland. (There is a separate National Trust for Scotland, which was set up in 1931.)

Furthermore, once a piece of land has come under National Trust ownership, it is difficult for its status to be altered. As a result of parliamentary legislation in 1907, the Trust was given the right to declare its property inalienable, so ensuring that in any subsequent dispute it can appeal directly to parliament.

As it works towards its dual aims of conserving areas of attractive countryside and encouraging greater public access (not easy to reconcile in this age of mass tourism), the Trust provides an excellent service for walkers by creating new concessionary paths and waymarked trails, maintaining stiles and footbridges and combating the ever-increasing problem of footpath erosion.

For details of membership, contact the National Trust at the address on page 94.

 ## Walkers and the Law

The average walker in a national park or other popular walking area, armed with the appropriate Ordnance Survey map, reinforced perhaps by a guidebook giving detailed walking instructions, is unlikely to run into legal difficulties, but it is useful to know something about the law relating to public rights of way. The right to walk over certain parts of the countryside has developed over a long period, and how such rights came into being is a complex subject, too lengthy to be discussed here. The following comments are intended simply as a helpful guide, backed up by the Countryside Access Charter, a concise summary of walkers' rights and obligations drawn up by the Countryside Commission.

Basically there are two main kinds of public rights of way: footpaths (for walkers only) and bridleways (for walkers, riders on horseback and pedal cyclists). Footpaths and bridleways are shown by broken green lines on Ordnance Survey

Holy Trinity church on the Avon at Stratford

Pathfinder and Outdoor Leisure maps and broken red lines on Landranger maps. There is also a third category, called byways: chiefly broad tracks (green lanes) or farm roads, which walkers, riders and cyclists have to share, usually only occasionally, with motor vehicles. Many of these public paths have been in existence for hundreds of years and some even originated as prehistoric trackways and have been in constant use for well over 2000 years. Ways known as RUPPs (roads used as public paths) still appear on some maps. The legal definition of such byways is ambiguous and they are gradually being reclassified as footpaths, bridleways or byways.

The term 'right of way' means exactly what it says. It gives right of passage over what, in the vast majority of cases, is private land, and you are required to keep to the line of the path and not stray on to the land on either side. If you inadvertently wander off the right of way – either because of faulty map-reading or because the route is not clearly indicated on the ground – you are technically trespassing and the wisest course is to ask the nearest available person (farmer or fellow walker) to direct you back to the correct route. There are stories about unpleasant confrontations between walkers and farmers at times, but in general most farmers are co-operative when responding to a genuine and polite request for assistance in route-finding.

Obstructions can sometimes be a problem and probably the most common of these is where a path across a field has been ploughed up. It is legal for a farmer to plough up a path provided that he restores it within two weeks, barring exceptionally bad weather. This does not always happen and here the walker is presented with a dilemma: to follow the line of the path, even if this inevitably means treading on crops, or to walk around the edge of the field. The latter course of action often seems the best but this means that you would be trespassing and not keeping to the exact line of the path. In the case of other obstructions which may block a path (illegal fences and locked gates etc), common sense has to be used in order to negotiate them by the easiest method – detour or removal. You should only ever remove as much as is necessary to get through, and if you can easily go round the obstruction without causing any damage, then you should do so. If you have any problems negotiating rights of way, you should report the matter to the rights of way department of the relevant council, which will take action with the landowner concerned.

Apart from rights of way enshrined by law, there are a number of other paths available to walkers. Permissive or concessionary paths have been created where a landowner has given permission for the public to use a particular route across his land. The main problem with these is that, as they have been granted as a concession, there is no legal right to use them and therefore they can be extinguished at any time. In practice, many of these concessionary routes have been established on land owned either by large public bodies such as the Forestry Commission, or by a private one, such as the National Trust, and as these mainly encourage walkers to use their paths, they are unlikely to be closed unless a change of ownership occurs.

Walkers also have free access to country parks (except where requested to keep away from certain areas for ecological reasons, eg. wildlife protection, woodland regeneration, safeguarding of rare plants etc), canal towpaths and most beaches. By custom, though not by right, you are generally free to walk across the open and uncultivated higher land of mountain, moorland and fell, but this varies from area to area and from one season to another – grouse moors, for

example, will be out of bounds during the breeding and shooting seasons and some open areas are used as Ministry of Defence firing ranges, for which reason access will be restricted. In some areas the situation has been clarified as a result of 'access agreements' between the landowners and either the county council or the national park authority, which clearly define when and where you can walk over such open country.

 ### The Ramblers' Association

No organisation works more actively to protect and extend the rights and interests of walkers in the countryside than the Ramblers' Association. Its aims are clear: to foster a greater knowledge, love and care of the countryside; to assist in the protection and enhancement of public rights of way and areas of natural beauty; to work for greater public access to the countryside; and to encourage more people to take up rambling as a healthy, recreational leisure activity.

It was founded in 1935 when, following the setting up of a National Council of Ramblers' Federations in 1931, a number of federations earlier formed in London, Manchester, the Midlands and elsewhere came together to create a more effective pressure group, to deal with such problems as the disappearance and obstruction of footpaths, the prevention of access to open mountain and moorland and increasing hostility from landowners. This was the era of the mass trespasses, when there were sometimes violent confrontations between ramblers and gamekeepers, especially on the moorlands of the Peak District.

Since then the Ramblers' Association has played an influential role in preserving and developing the national footpath

Ribbesford church surrounded by Wyre Forest

Countryside Access Charter

Your rights of way are:

- public footpaths – on foot only. Sometimes waymarked in yellow
- bridle-ways – on foot, horseback and pedal cycle. Sometimes waymarked in blue
- byways (usually old roads), most 'roads used as public paths' and, of course, public roads – all traffic has the right of way

Use maps, signs and waymarks to check rights of way. Ordnance Survey Pathfinder and Landranger maps show most public rights of way

On rights of way you can:

- take a pram, pushchair or wheelchair if practicable
- take a dog (on a lead or under close control)
- take a short route round an illegal obstruction or remove it sufficiently to get past

You have a right to go for recreation to:

- public parks and open spaces – on foot
- most commons near older towns and cities – on foot and sometimes on horseback
- private land where the owner has a formal agreement with the local authority

In addition you can use the following by local or established custom or consent, but ask for advice if you are unsure:

- many areas of open country, such as moorland, fell and coastal areas, especially those in the care of the National Trust, and some commons
- some woods and forests, especially those owned by the Forestry Commission
- country parks and picnic sites
- most beaches
- canal towpaths
- some private paths and tracks Consent sometimes extends to horse-riding and cycling

For your information:

- county councils and London boroughs maintain and record rights of way, and register commons
- obstructions, dangerous animals, harassment and misleading signs on rights of way are illegal and you should report them to the county council
- paths across fields can be ploughed, but must normally be reinstated within two weeks
- landowners can require you to leave land to which you have no right of access
- motor vehicles are normally permitted only on roads, byways and some 'roads used as public paths'

Further Information

---

network, supporting the creation of national parks and encouraging the designation and waymarking of long-distance routes.

Our freedom to walk in the countryside is precarious and requires constant vigilance. As well as the perennial problems of footpaths being illegally obstructed, disappearing through lack of use or extinguished by housing or road construction, new dangers can spring up at any time.

It is to meet such problems and dangers that the Ramblers' Association exists and represents the interests of all walkers. The address to write to for information on the Ramblers' Association and how to become a member is given on page 94.

Walking Safety

Although the reasonably gentle countryside that is the subject of this book offers no real dangers to walkers at any time of the year, it is still advisable to take sensible precautions and follow certain well-tried guidelines.

Always take with you both warm and waterproof clothing and sufficient food and drink. Wear suitable footwear, such as strong walking-boots or shoes that give a good grip over stony ground, on slippery slopes and in muddy conditions. Try to obtain a local weather forecast and bear it in mind before you start. Do not be afraid to abandon your proposed route and return to your starting point in the event of a sudden and unexpected deterioration in the weather.

All the walks described in this book will be safe to do, given due care and respect, even during the winter. Indeed, a crisp, fine winter day often provides perfect walking conditions, with firm ground and a clarity not offered at any other time of the year.

The most difficult hazard likely to be encountered is mud, especially along woodland and field paths, farm tracks and bridle-ways – the latter in particular can often get churned up by cyclists and horses. In summer, an additional difficulty may be narrow and overgrown paths, particularly along the edges of cultivated fields. Neither should constitute a major problem provided that the appropriate footwear is worn.

The Four Stones on the Clent Hills

Useful Organisations

Council for the Protection of Rural England
25 Buckingham Palace Road,
London SW1W 0PP
Tel. 0171 976 6433

Countryside Commission
John Dower House, Crescent Place,
Cheltenham, Gloucestershire GL50 3RA
Tel. 01242 521381
Birmingham Regional Office:
First Floor, Vincent House,
Tindal Bridge, 92-93 Edward Street,
Birmingham B1 2RA
Tel. 0121 233 9399

Forestry Commission
Information Branch,
231 Corstorphine Road,
Edinburgh EH12 7AT
Tel. 0131 334 0303
Long Distance Walkers' Association

10 Temple Park Close, Leeds, West
Yorkshire LS15 0JJ
Tel. 0113 264 2205

National Trust
Membership and general enquiries:
PO Box 39, Bromley, Kent BR1 3XL
Tel. 0181 315 1111
Severn Regional Office, Mythe End House,
Tewkesbury, Gloucestershire GL20 6EB
Tel. 01684 850051
Mercia Regional Office, Attingham Park,
Shrewsbury, Shropshire SY4 4TP.
Tel. 01743 709343

Ordnance Survey
Romsey Road, Maybush, Southampton
SO16 4GU
Tel. 0345 330011 (Lo-call)

Ramblers' Association
1–5 Wandsworth Road, London SW8 2XX
Tel. 0171 582 6878

Tourist Information Centres
Heart of England Tourist Board,
Woodside, Larkhill Road,
Worcester WR5 2EF
Tel. 01905 763436
Local tourist information offices:
Birmingham: 0121 643 2514

Coventry: 01203 832303/4
Kidderminster: 01562 829400
Redditch: 01527 60806
Shrewsbury: 01743 350761
Solihull: 0121 704 6130/4
Stafford: 01785 40204
Stratford-upon-Avon: 01789 293127
Telford: 01952 291370
Wolverhampton: 01902 312051
Worcester: 01905 726311/723471

Youth Hostels Association
Trevelyan House, 8 St Stephen's Hill, St
Albans, Hertfordshire AL1 2DY
Tel. 01727 855215

Ordnance Survey Maps of the Heart of England

The Heart of England is covered by
Ordnance Survey 1:50 000 scale ($1\frac{1}{4}$
inches to 1 mile or 2cm to 1km)
Landranger map sheets 126, 127, 128,
137, 138, 139, 140, 149, 150 and 151.
These all-purpose maps are packed with
information to help you explore the area.
Viewpoints, picnic sites, places of interest,
caravan and camping sites are shown, as
well as public rights-of-way information
such as footpaths and bridleways.

To examine the Heart of England in
more detail and especially if you are
planning walks, Ordnance Survey
Pathfinder maps at 1:25 000 scale ($2\frac{1}{2}$
inches to 1 mile or 4cm to 1km) are ideal.
Maps covering this area are:

810 (SK 04/14)	951 (SO 47/57)
827 (SJ 23/33)	952 (SO 67/77)
828 (SJ 43/53)	953 (SO 87/97)
890 (SJ 60/70)	954 (SP 07/17)
909 (SO 29/39)	955 (SP 27/37)
910 (SO 49/59)	973 (SO 66/76)
911 (SO 69/79)	975 (SP 06/16)
913 (SP 09/19)	997 (SP 05/15)
931 (SO 48/58)	998 (SP 25/35)
933 (SO 88/98)	1020 (SP 04/14)

Explorer maps 6 (Cannock Chase) and
14 (Malvern Hills), also at 1:25 000 scale
cover the area.

To get to the Heart of England, use the
Ordnance Survey Travelmaster map 7,
Wales and the West Midlands, at
1:250 000 scale (1cm to 2.5km or 1 inch
to 4 miles).

Ordnance Survey maps and guides are
available from most booksellers,
stationers and newsagents.

Dinham Bridge and Ludlow Castle

Entries in italics refer to illustrations